Dear Eric.
Yours an Eagle!.
Thanks!

Phil. $

Pasco County Library System
Overdue notices are a courtesy of the Library System.
Failure to receive an overdue notice does not absolve the borrower of the obligation to return the materials on time.

Horse Sense

The Key to Success Is Finding a Horse to Ride

by
Al Ries
Chairman, Trout & Ries

and

Jack Trout
President, Trout & Ries

McGraw-Hill, Inc.
New York St. Louis San Francisco Auckland Bogotá
Caracas Hamburg Lisbon London Madrid
Mexico Milan Montreal New Delhi Paris
San Juan São Paulo Singapore
Sydney Tokyo Toronto

Library of Congress Cataloging-in-Publication Data

Ries, Al.
   Horse Sense: the key to success is finding a horse to ride/ by Al Ries
and Jack Trout.
     p.   cm.
   ISBN 0-07-052735-0 :
   1. Success in business. 2. Job hunting. 3. Marketing.
I. Trout, Jack. II. Title.
HF5386.R5115   1991
650.14--dc20   90-13364
                                           CIP

1 2 3 4 5 6 7 8 9 0 DOC/DOC 9 8 5 4 3 2 1 0

ISBN   0-07-052735-0

The sponsoring editor for this book was William A. Sabin, the
editing supervisor was Barbara B. Toniolo, and the production
supervisor was Suzanne W. Babeuf. It was set in Baskerville by
McGraw-Hill's Professional Publishing composition unit.

Printed and bound by R. R. Donnelley & Sons Company.

*A sixty-minute audio program to accompany this book is now available.
Ask for it at your local bookstore.*

**Dedicated to the
most important, most difficult
marketing job of all . . .**

marketing yourself.

About the Authors

With their three previous books, *Positioning,
Marketing Warfare*, and *Bottom-Up Marketing*,
authors **Al Ries** and **Jack Trout** have firmly
established themselves as leading-edge thinkers
in the world of marketing products and services.
Horse Sense deals with the marketing of people.

The revolutionary ideas expressed here in
Horse Sense have taken shape over the past
decade, owing largely to a rigorous schedule of
speaking, writing, and consulting activities. Their
Greenwich, Connecticut, marketing strategy firm,
Trout & Ries, has developed tactics and strategies
for many of America's leading corporations,
including Burger King, IBM, AT&T, Humana,
Sotheby's, Paramount, Merck, and Warner-
Lambert.

Contents

Chapter 4. The medium shots

Chapter 5. The short shots

Chapter 6. The Company Horse

Chapter 7. The Product Horse

Chapter 8. The Idea Horse

Chapter 9. The Other-Person Horse

Chapter 10. The Partner Horse

Chapter 11. The Spouse Horse

Chapter 12. The Family Horse

Chapter 13. Changing horses

Chapter 14. There are no second acts

Chapter 15. Excuses, excuses

Introduction

Big Brother no longer cares.

Once upon a time, you signed on for a lifetime career at some big corporation. They trained you, they nurtured you, and they put you on a ladder to the top. How high you climbed the ladder was based on how hard you worked. Things were simple and foreseeable.

If you made only a modicum of mistakes, you would be successful and you could retire in glory. You didn't have to worry too much about your career. The company would do it for you. Justice would prevail. The harder you worked, the greater your chances of getting to the top. Diligence, patience, and loyalty were the highest corporate virtues.

That was yesterday.

In today's world of intense competition, restructurings, and corporate takeovers, it's become every person for himself. Or herself. You can't rely on the company to care of you because the company can't be sure it will be around to take care of you. You have to take care of yourself.

The age of competition has come sweeping through the business world. Companies are now competing on a global basis, and mistakes cost dearly.

On top of that, the wheeler-dealers and green-mailers arrived and started to "restructure" Corporate America.

No longer can companies carry extra people. "Lean" and "mean" are the watchwords of the day. No one is immune from the vagaries of takeovers or corporate raids.

The rash of corporate restructurings may partly explain employee malaise. In a recent survey, 51 percent of top executives say that their company has changed senior management and reorganized jobs in the past year or two. (Even that notorious revolving door, the federal government, revolves only once every four years.)

The bottom line: You can't depend on the company to take care of you. Big Brother is too busy trying to survive. To be successful today, you have to view yourself as a product rather than an employee. Your career is in your own hands, not in the hands of your friendly head of human resources.

Lifetime employment is no longer for life. The average college graduate today changes jobs three times in the first ten years out of school. (A sentence of "life in prison" today lasts for only eight years, on the average.) Indeed, people who spend their entire lives working for the same company are often disparagingly referred to as "tree-huggers."

As marketing strategists, we have watched, worked, and written about these turbulent times. The more we wandered around Corporate America, the more we realized that the traditional keys to success were no longer valid.

Trying harder, believing in yourself, and thinking positively are not steps up the ladder of success. As a matter of fact, success does not spring from anything inside yourself at all. Success is something given to you by others.

How to get others to make you successful is the theme of this book. Literally, you have to go out and market yourself.

Let's get one thing straight, however. This book is not a planning manual. There are no lists, no psychological exercises, no predictions of tomorrow's hot industries.

The purpose of this book is to shake you out of your concentration on yourself. We think you need to open your mind to the outside world. You need to search for success outside of yourself. This book will describe some of the people, places, things, and ideas where you can find it.

Losers look inside themselves for the key to success when success is all around them, needing only an open mind and a keen eye.

Winners look to others to make them successful. You have to know where to look and what to look for.

Good luck.

1

You're wrong, Norman Vincent

No book has had as much impact on establishing the principles of success as *The Power of Positive Thinking* by the Reverend Norman Vincent Peale.

"Formulate and stamp indelibly on your mind a mental picture of yourself as succeeding," said Dr. Peale. "Hold this picture tenaciously. Never permit it to fade. Your mind will seek to develop this picture."

If you believe the Norman Vincent Peales of this world, you are what you think. "Change your thoughts and you can change your world," states the Reverend Robert Schuller. In other words, unleash the power within you.

Is believing in yourself the key to success? We think not. We believe the key to real success in life is believing in someone else. In other words, find a horse to ride.

When you focus on yourself, you have only one ticket on the race. By expanding your horizon to include others, you greatly increase the odds in your favor. Furthermore, you open your mind to other possibilities besides people. The Product Horse, the Idea Horse, the Geography Horse, the Publicity Horse. Why settle on yourself with only one chance to win? Open your mind to thousands of other possibilities.

The believing-in-yourself theory of success

Look in a mirror and ask yourself, "Do I believe in that person who is looking back at me?"

Most of the experts think you don't. Which is why there are so many books on the power of positive thinking.

The Believe in Yourself and Make It Happen Guide by Dr. Connie Palladino is typical of the genre. "How much we earn is a report card that reflects how we see ourselves and how good we feel about ourselves," states Dr. Palladino, a career development consultant.

Los Angeles author Dave Grant flatly asserts: "Whatever you get paid is what you think you're worth. It's determined by your self-worth, your self-esteem." (Hey, McGraw-Hill, let's charge $100 for this book!)

What those and other experts have noticed is a high correlation between the elevated egos of this world and material success.

Success and self-confidence represent a chicken-and-egg problem with an answer. Actually, two answers.

Does self-confidence make you successful? Or does success make you self-confident?

Two yeses, in our opinion. But there's a big difference in the two approaches. To increase your own self-confidence is enormously difficult. It's like pushing on a string. You have to believe that most people with overactive egos were born that way. Donald Trump went to Norman Vincent Peale to get married, not to pump up his self-confidence.

Conversely, the self-doubters of this world either were born that way or acquired their insecurities in childhood. The classic mental illness of depression is perhaps an exaggerated form of self-doubt. (Try telling people who are depressed that all they have to do to get better is to increase their self-confidence.)

We believe you are born with a CQ as well as an IQ. A Confidence Quotient as well as an Intelligence Quotient. You can't really do much about raising either.

Yes, by all means, become more confident if you can. But do it the easier way. Become more successful and let success feed your self-confidence.

The setting-a-goal theory of success

Next to believing in yourself comes setting a goal. If you study the self-help books, you'll find that you can't be successful without one. First you start with a life goal. Then you set 5-year goals, 10-year goals, 15-year goals, etc.

If you study reality, you begin to wonder. If your goal was to be chief executive of a computer company, would you have spent the first 16 years of your working life with a cola company? Probably not. Yet that's what Apple chairman John Sculley did.

It works in the other direction too. If you wanted to own a pizza chain, would you have started out in computers, eventually taking the job of vice president of MIS at Pillsbury? That's what Herman Cain, president of Godfather's Pizza, did.

If you wanted to be Vice President of the United States at the age of 41, would you have spent four years in college drinking beer, playing golf, and getting grades of Cs and Ds? Dan Quayle did.

Dan Quayle's grandmother once told him, "You can be anything you want if you just try hard enough."

Not true. Dan Quayle didn't make Dan Quayle Vice President of the United States at the age of 41. George Bush did.

In our democratic egalitarian society, people have forgotten the classic definition of the road to success: It's not *what* you know that counts. It's *who* you know.

If you think that's a terrible way to run a country, you have company. So do we. It might be terrible, but it's also typical.

When you set a goal for yourself, you assume that your efforts alone will enable you to reach that goal. Very seldom is that true. You can't get to heaven all by yourself. You need a little help from God.

When you set a goal for yourself, you also put on "blinders." You miss opportunities which are not "in the main sequence." If you know where you're going, then you are not going to see the side road which often leads to the opportunity of a lifetime. You suffer from "tunnel vision."

Most people do. If there is one common mistake in marketing yourself, it is setting a personal goal and then failing to see other possibilities as they develop.

When you set a goal for yourself, you also take the mystery and excitement out of life. "If you always know exactly what you want," said Pablo Picasso, "that will be the most you'll ever find."

When you set a goal for yourself, you usually forget that others are setting goals too. If everybody wants to be king of the hill, the hill is going to get a little crowded. Try the valley instead.

According to *Playboy* magazine, 41 percent of American parents want a child of theirs to become President of the United States. With roughly 80 million families and two children per family, there are some 65 million kids with their eyes on Washington, D.C.

Look the other way.

Keep your options open. Don't lock yourself into a goal. For many people the future can be more exciting, more glamorous, and more rewarding than they could possibly imagine.

"I don't know where I'm going," said Daniel Richard Cooperman, 1989 graduate of Portledge Prep School on Long Island, "but I can't wait to get there."

Even after you have arrived, the road that took you there is never straight. "Life is a cobweb," said Ross Perot. "The lines cross at funny angles. Whether you're successful or not doesn't depend on how good your plans are, especially those five-year strategic plans business schools teach. Success depends on how you react to unexpected opportunities."

Tom Peters echos the same idea: "I don't like the whole notion of career planning. I've never had a formula, never had a life plan. I've taken advantage of luck when it came along." And he adds, "Luck is 98 percent of the deal."

Both Ross Perot and Tom Peters are iconoclasts.

They don't hesitate to attack traditional ideas. Most people, when they get to the top, proceed to cover their tracks. They never credit luck or being in the right place at the right time. Rather they credit hard work, setting goals, and believing in themselves.

They don't want you to know how they did it. It's a lot more satisfying to maintain the myth of merit. When you hear the head honcho or honcha give the speech about the wonderful opportunities that exist in the company for a person with ability who works hard, just say "Dan Quayle" ten times under your breath. It will keep your mind clear to recognize the real way up the ladder of success.

2

"Hey, Dad, how about $50 million?"

At a weight of 160, the late Sugar Ray Robinson was "pound for pound" the greatest boxer in the world.

At the age of 43, Donald Trump was "year for year" the most successful person in the world. (At the age of 44, of course, he was back down to earth again.)

Donald is smart, aggressive, personable. In fact, he has all the attributes anyone would ever need to get ahead in the world of business. Read his book *The Art of the Deal,* and he'll tell you how smart, aggressive, and personable he is.

One thing Mr. Trump left out of his book was the critical, make-or-break moment in his life, the moment when he turned to his father, Fred Trump, and asked: "Hey, Dad, how about $50 million?"

That's the message of this book. It doesn't matter how smart you are, how aggressive you are, and how personable you are. You'll do much, much better in life if you look outside yourself and find a horse to ride.

Even after Donald Trump was well on his way to the top, he never forgot what made him successful. When he was building his masterpiece, Trump Tower, he didn't neglect to say, "Hey, New York City, how about $50 million in tax abatements?"

And when his empire was tumbling down, Donald didn't hesitate to go to the bank and say, "Hey, Citibank, how about another $65 million?"

When the late Malcolm Forbes was asked to explain his own success, he said: "If you can pick a parent who owns a business, and be sure he's not mad at you when he checks out, it's a surer way to the top than anything else that comes to mind."

Malcolm's father used to say, "Son, what's the answer to ninety-nine questions out of a hundred? Money."

Unlike Malcolm Forbes and Donald Trump, most people weren't born with a golden spoon in their mouths. You probably don't have wealthy parents to turn to. No matter. The principle remains the same. To be a big success in life, you must find a horse to ride.

"I want to do it myself"

That's what Donald Trump could easily have said. "I want to go out into the world and *prove to myself* that I can be a big deal. I don't need my dad's money or his line of credit."

That's not uncommon. You hear it every day, especially from kids and teenagers. "I want to do it myself" is a daily refrain in most households with kids.

Some people never do grow up. They constantly try

to prove to themselves that they are smart and capable by striving for external success.

Using external success to buttress internal insecurities is a common condition of the human spirit. It accounts for the army of workaholics who populate most companies. The less they depend upon others, the more they can prove to themselves that they are really successful human beings.

People are me-oriented. What's the most popular spoken word in the English language? You guessed it. It's the word *I*. The second, third, and fourth most popular words are *me*, *my*, and *mine*.

You and *yours* aren't even in the top 20.

It's ironic. People turn inward when they should be turning outward. You can't be successful all by yourself. Other people make you successful. That's why you have to focus on other people, not yourself.

"How do I get to Carnegie Hall?" the tourist asked the hippie. "Practice, brother, practice," replied the hippie.

Our advice is just the opposite. Take a taxi.

Taking advantage of the bad things in life

Donald Trump took advantage of his good fortune to be born in a family with wealth. You can also take advantage of your bad fortune.

Ron Kovic came home from the Vietnam War in a wheelchair. Any previous goals he might have had for his life were left in the jungles of Southeast Asia.

Kovic became nationally known for protesting the Vietnam War on the floor of the 1972 Republican National Convention. After publication of his book *Born on the Fourth of July,* Kovic spoke at the Democratic National Convention in 1976 and served as a delegate in 1988.

His book led to the successful motion picture which he cowrote with director Oliver Stone.

"I really feel like one of the luckiest men on the face of the earth," says Ron Kovic. "I've wanted my life to stand for something important. I did not want to be thought of simply as someone who came home from a war with an injury, who people felt sorry for. I've always wanted to affect as many people as possible with my message."

What is success?

"Strange is our situation here upon earth," said Albert Einstein. "Each of us comes for a short visit, not knowing why, yet sometimes seeming to divine a purpose."

Some people want to *be* something. They want a title — like doctor, lawyer, dentist — that confers bragging rights on the holder. Others want to *do* something. They want to accomplish something with their lives.

Our sympathies lie with the latter. We admire people like Ron Kovic who want to matter, who want to leave their footprints in the sands of time.

Whatever success is, most people want it. A recent survey of affluent Americans, sponsored by Ernst & Young and Yankelovich Clancy Shulman, found that being successful was "very important" to two-thirds of the group. And these were people who make an average of $176,000 a year. (Only 14 percent of the group considered themselves to be "very well off.")

What is success? It's whatever you want it to be: money, power, position, recognition. It could be city hall; it could be Carnegie Hall. It could be CEO, CFO, or CIO.

Success is not mutually exclusive. You don't have to strive for one goal. Money, power, position, recognition, happiness, and friends usually go together.

But all things in moderation. Don't let success become a drug to feed your supercharged ego. A success addict can never get enough of anything: money, position, possessions. It's always one more Rolex watch or one more BMW and then I'll be happy.

Keep things in perspective. Actually, if you see success as something others do for you and not something you do for yourself, you are less likely to suffer from the insecurities of chasing success.

You're also in a good mental frame of mind to make use of the principles in this book. You're not hung up on a "Can Do" philosophy. Nobody can make you successful. Only *others* can do that for you. The Pope doesn't elect himself. Neither does the chairman of the board.

If you think this is a cold, crass, and conniving way to look at the game of life, you're right.

Cold, crass, conniving, and effective.

3

The long shots

What is your personal marketing strategy? Specifically, how do you propose to work your way up the ladder of life?

When you start with yourself and put the emphasis on self-confidence, you are assuming that success springs from inside yourself. To be successful, all you have to do is keep your nose to the grindstone and work hard.

If life were a horse race, you would be riding yourself. A horse that is mean, difficult, and unpredictable. Yet people often try to ride it. With very little success.

It is possible to succeed in the world of business or politics or life all by yourself. But it's not easy. And it's always foolhardy.

Like life itself, business is a social activity. As much cooperation as competition. So is government or social work or any other career you might be involved in.

Take selling, for example. You don't make a sale all by yourself. Somebody also has to buy what you're selling.

Remember, the winningest jockeys are not necessarily the lightest, the smartest, or the strongest. The best jockey doesn't necessarily win the race. The jockey that wins the race is usually the one with the best horse.

As a starter, let's handicap the horses, starting with the long shots. Why start with the long shots? Precisely because they are the most popular horses to ride.

They are also the most difficult and the least likely to pay off. (As the novice soon learns, the fastest way to lose money at the track is by betting on nothing but the long shots.)

When we quote the odds, we're not quoting the payoff. We're quoting your chances of winning big, your chances of becoming "successful" on your own terms. A long shot, unfortunately, doesn't pay off any better than a short shot. It's just a more difficult horse to win with.

The Hard-Work Horse: 100 to 1

The longest of shots is yourself. In our book, we quote the odds at 100 to 1.

When you build your personal marketing strategy around your own talents and abilities and neglect outsiders, you are riding yourself.

It's a tough proposition. You usually fall behind and then you start whipping yourself.

Whipping yourself is another way of saying "working harder." If everyone else is putting in seven hours a day, you put in eight. If everyone else puts in eight, you put in nine (with a little weekend work).

You know the pattern. Most people eagerly put in the extra time because they believe it is the *only* way to get ahead. In a recent survey by Steelcase, the office furniture company, 49 percent of office workers say they are working to their limits.

Not harder, mind you, but "working to their limits." There's a lot of whipping going on in the business race.

Robots, computers, and automation were supposed to reduce our work hours and give us more time for leisure. Sell your golf clubs. It's not happening. According to Louis Harris and Associates, the average American works 20 percent more today than in 1973 and has 32 percent less free time per week.

Managers work even longer hours. Sixty-five percent of top managers work more than 50 hours each week, according to the survey conducted by the American Productivity and Quality Center in Houston.

Top executives work the hardest. According to a *Wall Street Journal* survey, 88 percent of them work 10 or more hours a day. Eighteen percent work 12 or more hours a day.

It used to be if you worked hard, the boss would notice. "Here's a person who deserves a promotion." Now that everybody works hard, the way to get noticed is to leave at five and tell everybody you're so efficient you don't need to work late.

People who ride the Hard-Work Horse usually start slowly with an extra hour or two a week. When that doesn't bring a promotion or recognition, they get out the whip and accelerate their efforts. Pretty soon they are going flat out.

In reality, they might be way back in the pack with little chance to win the race. Yet they keep beating the Hard-Work Horse as if it were their only hope of reaching fame and fortune.

When what you are doing isn't working, you must do something different. This is one of the essential principles of marketing. When you are riding the Hard-Work Horse hell-bent for election, it's hard to say "Whoa." It's much easier to keep on working harder and harder.

Especially pathetic is the person who tries to save a loser by trying harder. Nobody tried as hard to save Eastern Airlines as Frank Borman. Yet all his efforts went for naught.

"If at first you don't succeed, try again," said W. C. Fields. "Then quit. No use in being a damn fool about it." We agree.

But don't successful people tend to work hard? Yes, they do. But that's a lot different from saying people who work hard tend to become successful.

The truth is, the higher you climb the ladder of life, the more fun the work is. You don't get to the top by working harder. But when you do get there, you might want to spend a little extra time enjoying the limos, the luncheons, the luxuries of expense-account living.

If you're not at the top and you still belong to the TGIM Club (Thank God It's Monday), you might think about changing your habits. Working harder dulls the mind and causes you to make mistakes. "I can do *almost* as much work in 11 hours as I can in 10," someone once said. If you work too long, you tend to make mistakes that take extra time to correct. Just because you have spent more time on a project doesn't necessarily mean you have done a better job. Less is often more, in labor as well as in architecture.

Some companies are beginning to see the light on

the issue of working after dark. They haven't started after-five inspections yet, but they are spelling out their philosophies.

Hard-driving Jack Welch, chairman of General Electric, is especially critical of the all-work-and-no-play policy of many managers. Says Jack: "If someone tells me, 'I'm working 90 hours a week,' I say, 'You're doing something terribly wrong. I go skiing on weekends. I go out with my buddies on Friday and party. You've got to do the same or you've got a bad deal. Put down a list of the 20 things you're doing that make you work 90 hours, and 10 of them have to be nonsense.'"

Chris Whittle echoes the same idea. Whittle is chief executive officer of Whittle Communications, a $185 million company based in Knoxville, Tennessee. (In 1988 he sold 50 percent of his company to Time Inc. for $185 million.)

"Entrepreneurs work far too hard," says Chris Whittle. "I squandered large parts of my twenties and thirties in needless, completely neurotic work. I got tangled up in the myth of the hard-charging, hard-working, we'll-stay-here-till-we-drop entrepreneur. That's a very destructive attitude. It's unnecessary. It's unhealthy. And you can have entrepreneurial success without it."

Whittle is known as an "idea" generator. He created an uproar with *Channel One,* a television program for high school students that carries news (and commercials) into the classroom. He also created *Special Reports,* a glossy magazine distributed free to doctors for their waiting rooms.

Hard work and a good horse will get you anything in life. The hard work is optional.

The IQ Horse: 75 to 1

In the dairy, cream rises to the top. In daily life, it's generally not true.

It's mostly milk at the top of the corporate bottle. You would be appalled if you gave IQ tests to the chief executive officers of *Fortune* 500 companies. The professors at any decent community college would score higher.

We're not critical of the boards of directors that picked these CEOs. Intelligence is a two-edged sword. Too little and you can't cope with the corporate paperwork: writing memos, making travel arrangements, filling out expense accounts. Too much and you get out of touch with reality. You suffer from the absent-minded professor syndrome.

Top executives come from the middle of the IQ curve. As the college president said to the faculty, "Be nice to your A students because they'll come back and be your colleagues, but be exceptionally nice to your B and C students because they will come back and give us a new auditorium and a new science building."

Peter McColough, former chairman of Xerox, made the same point about his Harvard Business School class of 1949. "The record of accomplishment corresponds negatively with the standing of the class," McColough reported. "The top people did not do that well. The middle third did. The guys who got the highest marks tended to be in the middle in accomplishment."

If you believe good grades are the key to success, be sure to attend your twenty-fifth high school reunion.

Success in the classroom and success in the boardroom seem to have little to do with each other.

There's a reason why intelligence doesn't correlate very well with success. The smarter people are, the more they depend upon themselves. After all, they know everything. They depend on themselves to get ahead. But it's a long shot.

Less intelligent people know they are less intelligent. Therefore, they are more likely to look for others to help them up the ladder.

There's nothing wrong with being smart. It can't hurt you if you maintain your perspective. But look for another horse to ride.

The Education Horse: 60 to 1

Related to IQ is the issue of education. Should you depend on the Education Horse to get you to the top?

Well, the Education Horse is particularly good out of the starting gate. We think you should get yourself a brand-name education at places like Harvard, Princeton, Yale, Duke, Stanford, or Northwestern. You won't learn any more than you would at your local state university. But you will get a brand name that will help you ride through the employment departments of most companies.

All by itself, a college degree doesn't buy you very much. Today, college graduates account for approximately 25 percent of the U.S. work force, a higher percentage than in any other country in the world. And the proportion of college graduates continues to increase. Fifty-nine percent of all high school graduates now go on to college.

As college degrees become more common, the brand name increases in value. This is why the Ivy League schools are a particularly rich source of future chief executives. According to a recent survey of *Fortune* 500 companies, nearly 19 percent of current CEOs hold Ivy League degrees.

But don't let your degree raise your ego level. "The world is full of educated derelicts," said Ray Kroc, who built McDonald's with very few college graduates, including himself. Even today, more than half of all McDonald's corporate executives never graduated from college.

Remember the function of the Education Horse is to get you into the race. A degree all by itself is unlikely to make your horse go any faster.

Be careful riding the Education Horse. You can easily lose your most precious commodity in the halls of ivy. As the old saying goes, "You are born with common sense and then you go to school and lose it."

Furthermore, in many big companies, you'll never rise to the top by flaunting an advanced degree. This is especially true in the megacorporations where Ph.D.s belong in the research department.

Dr. John Francis Welch, Jr., didn't get to be chief executive of the fifth largest U.S. industrial company, with sales in 1988 of almost $50 billion, by riding his Ph.D. Rather he hid his Ph.D., dropped the Jr., and adopted the more plebian name of Jack.

The Company Horse: 50 to 1

In the past this was the horse to ride. A college-graduate-to-be would interview with a number of big companies on campus, hopefully getting a number of job offers. Normally you'd pick the biggest company or the highest starting salary, preferably both.

Once that decision was made, you were set for the rest of your life. It was ever onward and upward, with the CEO prize a reasonable possibility.

No more. The way to the top of most companies is filled with more twists and turns than a bowl of spaghetti. Ability is probably the least important attribute in your personal marketing arsenal.

A company, especially a big company, might not represent much of a future to you, but it does have one major benefit. A big, well-known company is a great place to get your ticket punched, provided it's the *right* big company.

Today's with-it yuppie will often have graduated from a carefully selected brand-name college (hopefully Harvard), will wear carefully selected brand-name clothing (Ralph Lauren Polo, to be sure), will drive a carefully selected brand-name car (BMW, of course), will drink carefully selected brand-name liquor (Absolutly), and then work for a company that no one has ever heard of.

When asked why, your otherwise with-it yuppie will often say, "They made me the best offer."

Money is not the best measure of a job's potential. Kennedy was wrong. Ask not what you can do for your company. Ask what your company can do for you.

Why do you suppose junk bonds pay the highest interest rates? The same reason junk companies pay the highest salaries.

Watch out for the junk companies of the business world. Not only won't they do anything for you; they will often do permanent damage to your long-term career.

No matter how brilliant you are, it never pays to cast your lot with a loser. The best officer on the Titanic wound up in the same lifeboat as the worst. And that's if he was lucky enough to stay out of the water.

In particular, watch out for the blue chips of the corporate world that are beginning to lose their luster. General Motors, IBM, Xerox. These former high-fliers are on the decline. They are a lot easier to recognize than you might think. In some cases, they have had a decade or more of decay.

No company goes belly up overnight. Even the Titanic stayed afloat for three hours after hitting the iceberg.

You don't have to be a financial or marketing genius to spot a long-term loser. The lifeboats have been leaving companies like Western Union for years. The New York Central was losing ground for a decade or longer before the company went bankrupt.

Yet many prospective employees don't want to see the danger signals. All too often their egos get in the way. Not only do losers-in-the-making pay more; they seem to offer more opportunity. "I can be a hero," the new employee thinks. "I can help turn them around."

The last time we counted, IBM had 387,112 employees. Do you think Employee No. 387,113 will make much of a difference?

There's an exception to every rule. Chrysler Corporation had 150,000 employees when Lee Iacocca arrived in 1978. But Iacocca arrived as president with a mandate to turn things around. So if you get the urge to join a loser, make sure you join in a position of authority with a clear-cut commitment from the board of directors for making changes.

The time to ride the Company Horse is early. Four of the first ten men to be drafted into the U.S. Army during World War II ended up as officers. None of the last ten did.

Companies like Apple, Digital Equipment, and Xerox spawned a host of millionaires among their early employees. The pickings were slim for later arrivals.

How do you spot a megacorporation in its foaling stage? You don't. You look for another person, a product, or an idea that seems to have a future.

You'll find these horses described more fully in the chapters that follow.

4

The medium shots

What differentiates a medium shot from a long shot?

The long shots are based on finding something inside yourself. The medium shots are also based on using something inside yourself, but with a difference. You have to connect that concept with others.

The Creativity Horse: 25 to 1

What if you're born with talent? What if you're a natural artist, writer, or musician?

Good luck. You're going to need it. "Full many a flower is born to blush unseen, and waste its sweetness on the desert air," wrote Thomas Gray.

Full many a talented flower has wilted in the harsh world of reality since Gray wrote those lines in 1750 in a country graveyard. To be a creative star, you need more than talent. You need recognition.

How do you get someone else to recognize your ability? If you're an artist, you need a gallery to recognize your ability. If you're a writer, you need a publisher. If you're a musician, you need a record company.

In short, you need recognition from someone else who can make you successful. You need a horse to ride.

Our best advice is to expose yourself to as many galleries, publishers, record companies as you can find. And remember, you don't need to please the herd. You just need one horse to ride.

Paul McCartney failed the audition for the Cathedral Choir in his hometown of Liverpool. The key to McCartney's success was Brian Epstein. He found the Fab Four and molded them, often against their wishes, into a world-class act.

Times change. Today Paul McCartney is composing an hour-long cantata commissioned (would you believe) by the Liverpool Cathedral Choir.

John Lennon, the most influential songwriter of his generation, gave the aunt who raised him a gold plaque engraved with her oft-repeated words, "You'll never make a living playing that guitar." Without Brian Epstein, it's unlikely that Lennon would have ever made a living playing his guitar.

If you were born with creative talent, then ask yourself this question: "Brian, where are you?"

Creative talents also have to learn how to listen to their audiences. They have to adapt to what people want them to be, rather than vice versa.

A young singer with a fine soprano voice (augmented by many singing lessons) was assigned to perform *The End of a Perfect Day* for admiring relatives. When his adolescent voice cracked and broke at the family gathering, he discovered he had the ability to make people laugh. The singer-turned-comedian was Bob Hope.

The goal-oriented individual would have said, "I'm not going to let this incident stop me from becoming a professional singer." The hard-work-oriented individual would have said, "I have to practice more."

Accidents will happen. Successful people take advantage of accidents. Unsuccessful people are usually "inside"-oriented. They don't listen.

Another famous comedian started his career as a musician. Jack Benny took violin lessons with the hope of becoming a concert performer. He started in vaudeville as a violinist before switching to stand-up comedy routines.

After creative people become successful, they often resist being type-cast. They want to be free to try many different things. A movie star wants to star in many different roles, from comedy to tragedy. A singer wants to sing many different types of songs. A writer wants to write a wide range of articles, books, screen plays, etc. Everyone wants to be a Renaissance man or woman.

Don't resist. The best rule for success is to become type-cast. Arnold Schwarzenegger gets $8 million to make a motion picture. Can you imagine how much less he would make if he could act?

It's true of Jack Benny and Bob Hope too. Their carefully cultivated public stereotypes made them worth millions. Marilyn Monroe, John Wayne, Clint Eastwood: the bigger the star, the narrower the focus. In truth, the biggest, richest stars become cardboard cutouts or cartoons of themselves.

It's true in business too. Sandy Sigoloff is known as a turnaround artist. You might say he is *the* turnaround expert. Ming the Merciless he is called, after the Flash Gordon villain. The name fits. He'll cut costs, lay off thousands, liquidate subsidiaries, anything to save a company from going down the drain.

Sigoloff has made millions from his narrow "turn-around artist" focus. His reputation has been burnished in articles in *Business Week, Fortune, Forbes, The Wall Street Journal,* and hundreds of other magazines and newspapers. So how many companies has Ming the Merciless turned around? A hundred? Fifty? Twenty-five? Ten?

How about three? Republic Corporation, a Los Angeles-based conglomerate; Daylin Corporation, a $600 million Los Angeles retailer; and The Wickes Companies, the nation's largest retailer of lumber and building materials. Currently Sandy Sigoloff is trying his magic on L. J. Hooker, the troubled U.S. subsidiary of Hooker Corp. of Australia.

We're not denigrating Mr. Sigoloff. Four in a row would be a spectacular achievement. (Roughly equivalent to Joe Montana in Super Bowls, for example.) With a narrow focus you don't need many victories to become a legend in your own time. In some cases, one is enough.

Bruce McKinnon is also a turnaround artist, but on a smaller scale. Just 33 years old, McKinnon specializes in revitalizing cable television systems. He's on his third such assignment, each time increasing his salary 25 to 50 percent.

If you're going to ride the Creativity Horse, you'll go farther if you have a personal trademark that's offbeat. It could be long hair (the Beatles) or an upturned mustache (Salvador Dali) or a white suit (Tom Wolfe).

If you want people to think you are creative, you have to *look* creative.

Walk into an advertising agency. You can easily tell the creative people from everybody else. The creative people are the ones in blue jeans. The suits and dresses are worn by account and media people. Art directors, because they are considered more creative than mere writers, have to go a step or two further. (The current state-of-the-art look for a male art director, for example, is ponytail and earrings.)

Nicknames also help communicate the creativity message. Ming the Merciless, Elvis the Pelvis, Madonna. People with names like that must be creative.

Short nicknames are even more powerful. The Boss (Bruce Springsteen). The Chairman (Frank Sinatra). The King (Clark Gable).

Awards are also helpful to establish a creative reputation. In some industries, you must have certain awards before you are taken seriously. In the advertising industry, it's a Clio. In the motion picture industry, it's an Oscar. You get further in your own industry if you can manage not only to win an award but also to flaunt it.

Shelley Winters was asked to try out for a part in a Robert De Niro movie. When she arrived at the audition, she pulled an Oscar out of her purse and put it on the table. She opened her purse again and put a second Oscar on the table. "Some people think I can act," purred Ms. Winters. "Do I still have to audition?"

She got the part.

The Creativity Horse is a difficult creature to ride, mainly because riders get their priorities reversed. They assume that "talent will out" when all that talent buys you is a ticket in the lottery. More than almost any other horse, the Creativity Horse demands outside recognition for success.

That outside recognition sometimes never arrives. Vincent Van Gogh painted hundreds of pictures in his lifetime, yet sold only one. Van Gogh called himself "a poor bungler who can't sell a picture."

Ninety-nine years after he killed himself, one of his paintings, "Portrait of Dr. Gachet," was sold to a Japanese collector for $82.5 million.

Don't beat your head against a brick wall (or cut off one of your protuberances) if your talent isn't immediately recognized. As a matter of fact, expect that it won't be. The essence of your problem is outside recognition. Whether you write, paint, act, sing, dance, photograph, or what-have-you, spend a good portion of your time searching for the outside expert who can certify your creativity.

If you really want to be a big creative success, go overboard on the outsiders the way Harvey Mackay did.

Mackay was 54 years old when he wrote his first book, *Swim With the Sharks Without Being Eaten Alive*. But he didn't spend all of this time writing or swimming. Much of it was spent getting endorsements.

Including Robert Redford, Ted Koppel, Mario Cuomo, Gloria Steinem, Gerald Ford, Walter Mondale, Peter Ueberroth, Eddie Albert, Lou Holtz, Bob Knight, Al McGuire, Fran Tarkenton, Stan Smith, Charles Schwab, Warren (rent-a-car) Avis, Abigail (Dear Abby) Van Buren, Billy Graham, and of course Norman Vincent Peale.

Also including the CEOs of United Airlines, 7-Eleven Stores, Porsche, Estée Lauder, Playtex, ConAgra,

Northwestern Bell, IDS, Dayton-Hudson, Carlson Companies, Cray Research, Farley Industries, Dresher, Ushio Electric, and The Stanley Works.

In addition, Mackay lined up the presidents of Stanford, Brown, and Kansas State Universities. Plus the president of the Menninger Foundation and former presidents of General Motors and G. D. Searle.

There were also endorsements by four authors, including Kenneth Blanchard, coauthor of *The One Minute Manager,* who wrote the foreword.

How successful was *Swim With the Sharks?* (Do you really have to ask?) The book broke all sorts of publishing records with a run of more than 40 weeks on *The New York Times* best-seller list. It sold 2.3 million copies, enough to rank among the ten top-selling business titles of all time. Currently Harvey Mackay makes a million dollars a year on the lecture circuit, not including royalties.

How well written was *Swim With the Sharks?* Read the book and decide. Then ask yourself the question, "Does it really matter?" How good a singer is Madonna?

If you just want to be creative, spend all your time with yourself working on your "art" the way Van Gogh did. If you want to be creative and successful, spend part of your time on your "art" and part of your time on selling yourself to other people. The way Mackay did.

Never forget that in the world of creativity, as in the world itself, it's other people that make you successful. It's the art critic that makes the artist successful. It's the movie critic that makes the movie producer successful.

Nine times out of ten, your own ego gets in the way. People want to be recognized for their creative ability, not their sales ability. Ask yourself, "Does it really matter?"

To many people it does. First and foremost, they want to believe in themselves. They want to feel "creative." That's the other side of the coin. If "heads" is the power of positive thinking, "tails" is the self-destructive aspect of not believing in yourself.

Sidestep the issue. Believe in the power of others. They are the only people that can make you successful. Whether you believe in yourself or not has no bearing on the issue.

When you sell your creativity to others, remember the package is as important as the product. Would *Swim With the Sharks* have made it to the best-seller list with the more prosaic title of *Getting Ahead in Business?*

Probably not.

Would a book with the bland title of *Marketing Yourself* go anywhere?

Probably not. The package is just as important as the product. That's why we changed the name of this book to *Horse Sense.*

Would you spend $19.95 for a copy of a book entitled *Leadership Secrets?*

Probably not. Yet hundreds of thousands of people spent that kind of money for *Leadership Secrets of Attila the Hun* by Wess Roberts.

The package is just as important as the product. Sometimes more important.

The Hobby Horse: 20 to 1

Maybe what you do on vacation and what you do as a vocation ought to be the same thing. Look at what

Hugh Hefner accomplished without leaving his bedroom. And what Helen Gurley Brown accomplished with her book *Sex and the Single Girl*, which led to the job of editor in chief of *Cosmopolitan* magazine.

It's amazing how many successful businesses have evolved out of avocations or hobbies.

Paul Prudhomme loves to eat and his 300 pounds show it. So he turned his hobby into the world-famous New Orleans restaurant K. Paul's Kitchen.

One of the factors that come into play is confidence. When you like to do something, you tend to do a lot of it. The more you do it, the better you get at it and the more confidence you develop. (How do you get to be a good speaker? You make a lot of speeches.)

Note the reversal of conventional wisdom. Success breeds confidence. Confidence doesn't breed success, unless you are particularly fond of fooling yourself. (As in the old expression, "He's a legend in his own mind.")

How do you turn a hobby into an executive position? You keep your eyes open. Eduardo Stern is a Chilean architect by training and a ski nut by avocation. So when he learned that two French companies were planning to build a world-class ski resort outside Santiago, Chile, he was the natural choice to run it.

Valle Nevado is destined to be one of the world's biggest ski resorts. Total investment planned: $350 million.

How do you turn a hobby into a fortune? You could have spent $100 for a membership in the National Football League when it was founded in 1920 in Ralph Hay's Hupmobile showroom in Canton, Ohio. (The Dallas NFL franchise was just sold for $150 million.)

More recently, at a regular meeting of a group of New York City food fanatics, someone complained how hard it was to find a really good restaurant.

Tim Zagat, a lawyer for Gulf + Western, had a bright idea. Why not survey the group's friends and circulate a newsletter listing their favorites? In a moment of Bordeaux-inspired bravado, Zagat volunteered to organize the project.

Requests for Zagat's photocopied survey soon grew to the point that his wife Nina, also an attorney, suggested that they start selling the guide to cover expenses.

Ten years after that fateful dinner, the Zagat guide has become the top-selling restaurant book in New York City. Tim Zagat is no longer a practicing lawyer but the mogul of a growing mini-empire of restaurant and hotel guides across the United States.

For New York City gourmets, the annual appearance of the Zagat survey has become an event on a par with the Parisian introduction of the new *Guide Michelin*.

Over the years, the Zagat guides have earned the Zagats millions of dollars.

In the case of Tim Zagat, it's easy to see how a goal can get in the way of success. Let's say that Mr. Zagat wanted to be in charge of the legal department of a *Fortune* 500 company.

So why fool around with a restaurant guide? You can't eat your way to the top.

Mike Sinyard's hobby is biking. Every workday at 11 a.m., 40-year-old Sinyard dons cycling clothes, hops on his bike, and rides 20 miles. As many as 50 of his employees at Specialized Bicycle Components Inc. ride with him on the two-hour trip.

Founded by bike enthusiasts rather than business-people, Specialized spotted the appeal of fat-tired mountain bikes and began producing them in 1981. Today the company does $80 million in sales and is considered a market leader in the booming mountain-bike category.

How do you turn a hobby into a business? Bob McKnight liked to surf more than anything else. So in 1976 he teamed up with world champion surfer Jeff Hakman to sell "boardshorts" out of the back of a van.

Today their company, Quicksilver Inc., has an annual volume of $50 million selling clothes for the surfing set. The company maintains a surfing sense of humor. A sign on President Bob's door says "Robert B. McKnight, Jr., Director of Groovology."

The Geography Horse: 15 to 1

When you're considering a career, the options are endless. There are big companies, small companies. Private companies, public companies. Business, government, education. Managerial occupations, professional occupations.

You can work with your mind or with your hands, or you can work with both (as a surgeon does). There are indoor occupations, outdoor occupations. Big-city opportunities, small-town opportunities. How do you begin to select from this vast array of possibilities?

Maybe you don't. Maybe opportunity lies more in dealing with the environment you find yourself in and less in searching the world for the perfect occupation in the perfect company in the perfect location.

Perfection in infinite time is worth zero.

Designer Toni Silver loves to travel. In 1987 she found herself in Bali where she had gone for a vacation. She fell in love with the Balinese people, the Balinese culture, the Balinese food. She stayed two months.

Using native prints, Toni Silver created a line of shirts, bomber jackets, and trousers. She also located a Bali factory that could produce her designs.

Called Silverwear, the clothes have become a big success at exclusive shops in New York and Boston. Silverwear could turn out to be a gold mine for Toni Silver. (If not, she could always take another trip.)

Rachel Crespin returned from a trip to Turkey with a shearling coat that her friends admired so much they sent her to designers like Calvin Klein and Donna Karan. Pretty soon she developed a business as an intermediary between American designers and Turkish factories. She also designs coats which are on sale at places like Bergdorf Goodman and Saks Fifth Avenue.

Pearl Sydenstricker's parents were Presbyterian missionaries on the Yangtse River in China. She learned to speak Chinese before she could speak English. After graduating from Randolph-Macon College in Virginia, she returned to China. Three years later she married Dr. John Buck, an agricultural specialist whose work took him to Nanking in rural China. There she gathered much of the material she used in her novel, *The Good Earth*.

The book was an immediate success, winning the Pulitzer Prize as the best novel of 1931. It spent almost two years on the best-seller list, was translated into more than 30 languages, and became the basis of a successful motion picture. Pearl S. Buck went on to become the first woman to win a Nobel Prize in literature.

What Buck found in China, Blattner is finding in Zaire. Fresh out of Syracuse University, Edwyn Blattner joined his father's business, a modest textile mill in Kinshasa, Zaire.

Over the next few years, with leverage and luck, he bought a succession of other businesses: Kinshasa's only slaughterhouse; a Goodyear tire factory; a canning mill; and rubber, coffee, and palm oil plantations.

He also bought land at bargain prices. The family now owns 60,000 square miles (an area larger than the state of New York) spread throughout Zaire.

The Blattner family organization, African Holding Company of America, consists of 40 entities employing 17,000 workers. The largest and most striking properties were developed by Edwyn Blattner, now just 33 years old.

"He's just like that American, Donald Trump, but even more so," said a Zairian businessman who has traveled widely in the West. "What he's been able to do here in such a brief time is phenomenal."

Geography was also behind the success of Peter Main, a Canadian working for a Japanese company in the United States. But the key to Main's success was his house in Vancouver in the seventies, where his neighbor was Minoru Arakawa. Over the years, the two kept in touch.

In the eighties, when Minoru Arakawa was trying to get a new video game company started in the United States, he began prodding his old neighbor to join him. In late 1986, just as the company was finishing its first test market, Main agreed.

Main's timing was superb. Three years later, the

video game company (Nintendo) had captured 80 percent of a $2.6 billion market. Peter Main, the 48-year-old vice president of marketing, was named "Marketer of the Year" by *Adweek* magazine.

Why did Arakawa pick Main? "His background is not toys or electronic products," says Minoru Arakawa. "But I believe common sense is more important than experience." Also important is living in the right neighborhood.

Success is where you find it. Don't waste time looking for exactly the right place, the right environment. You won't find it. And even if you did, you probably wouldn't recognize it.

Success in life begins with acceptance. Accept the things that can't be changed or are perhaps too difficult to change. Then start to change the one thing you have total control over. Yourself.

The Publicity Horse: 10 to 1

It's a fact of corporate life, especially in big corporations, that *visibility* counts for more than *ability*. (It's nice to have both, but if you have to take one or the other, take *visibility*.)

You can ride the Publicity Horse to the top because 90 percent of the people are not independent thinkers. Ninety percent believe only what they read in the paper, hear on the radio, see on television ... or what other people tell them. And where do these other people get their ideas? Of course, from what they read in the paper, hear on the radio, or see on television.

The Publicity Horse is powerful, but it also works in reverse. Negative publicity can destroy a product, a company, or a person. Ask Joseph Hazelwood, the former captain of the Exxon Valdez.

Nor is it the volume of publicity that counts. What you should strive for is to generate one powerful positive story that you can repeat over and over again.

"I liked the Remington razor so much, I bought the company." Have you ever read a story on Victor Kiam that *doesn't* mention the fact that he liked the razor so much he bought the company? Of course not. That one idea is so powerful he can ride it forever.

Benito Mussolini was prime minister of Italy for 21 years. Do you know any positive thing about Signor Mussolini except that he made the trains run on time?

One idea. That's what you should look for to attach to your name. Walter Weir was a copywriter who founded an advertising agency called West, Weir & Bartels. The best word he ever wrote was in describing himself as a "wordsmith." Many stories appeared in the advertising trade press about "wordsmith Walter Weir."

Ed McCabe is another Madison Avenue copywriter of note. (Volvo cars, Perdue chicken.) A number of years ago Mr. McCabe was elected to the Advertising Copywriters' Hall of Fame. From that day on, nearly every story referred to him as "hall-of-famer Ed McCabe." Not a bad word to own.

Bess Myerson was voted Miss America in 1944. So how does every story refer to her? "Former Miss America Bess Myerson." Not exactly a bad set of words to own, especially if you are 62 years old.

There's a trade secret among reporters that helps explain why a simple idea tends to get repeated over and over again. You might think that reporters start a story from scratch. But they don't, especially in today's computer-oriented society.

Reporters use their PCs to pull up other stories on the same subject from their own and other publications. They extract the essence of your identity from previous stories. Heaven help you if "ex-convict" or something similar ever gets attached to your name. (Heaven can't help you, but the judicial system can; change your name.)

If you plan to ride the Publicity Horse, first get yourself a word or an idea.

What word do you own? Publicity is not an easy horse to ride. You have to be ruthless in discarding material so that you can focus on one idea or concept.

David Liederman owns cookies. His big break came on July 25, 1979, in *The New York Times* with an article entitled "The Search for the Best Chocolate-Chip Cookie in New York." Florence Fabricant, the writer of the piece, liked David's chocolate-chip cookie better than anyone else's. The rest, as they say, is cookie history.

Where would David be without Florence's article?

Frieda Caplan owns Kiwi. As a matter of fact, she is known as the "Queen of Kiwi."

In the sixties she introduced the Chinese gooseberry to the United States, but renamed it "kiwifruit" after the bird native to New Zealand where the fruit originated.

Frieda's Finest Produce Company in Los Angeles is the first wholesale produce house in the country to be founded, owned, and operated by a woman. It does $20 million a year.

Interesting fact. Frieda Caplan never flew to the Far East looking for exotic fruit. She sat in her office and it walked in the front door.

One day a Safeway produce buyer asked her if she had ever heard of a fruit called the Chinese gooseberry. A Safeway customer had asked about it. Frieda had never seen one but promised to keep an eye out. Six months later, by sheer coincidence, a broker stopped by and offered her a load of Chinese gooseberries.

Frieda's cardinal rule: "Always have an open door. Always listen to what anyone has to offer."

Good publicity ideas are like that. They often walk in the front door, and they are usually invented by others.

To ride the Publicity Horse well, you have to learn how to "play the press." You can't be too aggressive and you can't be too bashful. As a general rule, don't call them. Let them call you.

But why would a reporter or television assignment editor call you? First you have to expose yourself by making a speech or writing an article. And to give yourself a chance to make the publicity big-time, you have to be slightly outrageous.

It's the offbeat, shocking, or controversial idea that will get the attention of the media. Nobody wants to do a story on motherhood or apple pie.

Andy Warhol was a master publicity jockey. Everything he did, from his appearance to his artwork to his social life, was designed to make media waves the only way possible. You have to "shock" your way into the news.

The Wall Street Journal recently devoted 10 column inches on the front page of its marketing section to a 56-page book entitled *Mafia Management*. Written by Hector Davila, it is priced at an outrageous $59.95.

Everything Madonna does, from her name to her

videos, is outrageous, including her income last year which was $23 million. (Frank Sinatra made only $14 million.) How much money did you make last year? And you're worried about what you're going to wear to the office? Wear the green suit with the red tie.

Howard Stern makes a million a year on New York radio with language more appropriate to a locker room in the NFL.

At the same time, many English-teacher types are out looking for work.

The short shots

What's the difference between a short shot and a medium shot?

In a medium-shot situation, you depend partially on yourself and partially on outsiders. In a short-shot situation, you depend totally on outsiders for your success.

When you get totally outside of yourself, the odds ,et better. Here are the six most important short shots. You might think of these as the favorites in the marketing race.

The Product Horse: 5 to 1

The best example of riding a product to the top is Lee Iacocca. According to the 1986 Gallup Poll, Iacocca was the second-most-admired person in the world, just behind Ronald Reagan and ahead of the Pope.

Everyone knows the story of how Lee Iacocca was fired by Henry Ford II as president of Ford and how he went on to become a living legend at Chrysler. But how did Mr. Iacocca get to be president of Ford?

In a word, Mustang.

Mustang was the horse Iacocca rode to the top. Did Iacocca design the Mustang? No. Did he engineer the Mustang? No. Did he recognize the merits of somebody else's design? Yes, and that was Iacocca's ticket to the top.

Recognizing somebody else's genius is almost always the key to your own success. Seven full-sized clay models were assembled in the outdoor viewing area at the Ford Design Center.

Iacocca picked the design executed by Joe Oros, Gail Halderman, and L. David Ash. "It was the only one in the courtyard that seemed to be moving," he said later.

"The hottest car in the auto business today is Ford's Mustang, and the hottest executive in the business is Ford Division General Manager Lee Iacocca," reported *Forbes* magazine in September 1964.

When you get your day in the courtyard, don't think it's going to be easy. Most people can't recognize a good product idea when they see one.

The McDonald brothers opened their drive-in in December 1948. Hundreds of thousands of people bought McDonald's hamburgers before Ray Kroc arrived on the scene five years later.

Did any of these customers recognize what they had just seen? If so, the record doesn't show it. McDonald's wasn't just a place to save 10 cents on a hamburger. It was also an opportunity to make millions.

Ray Kroc did. He recognized the brilliance of the McDonald's concept and made hundreds of millions from it.

Nor was Ray Kroc particularly quick out of the starting gate. He didn't sell his first hamburger until he was 52 years old.

It's instructive to compare Dick and Mac McDonald with Ray Kroc. The brothers *invented* the product concept, and Ray Kroc *recognized* the potential of the concept. Who made the big bundle? The inventor or the recognizer?

As an inventor Ray Kroc was a loser. His menu suggestions consistently flopped. One lame idea: the Hulaburger, a slice of grilled pineapple and two pieces of cheese in a bun. All-time favorites like the Big Mac and the Egg McMuffin were proposed by franchisees.

Be a recognizer. Look outside yourself for the product that can make your fortune.

What the 15-cent hamburger did for Ray Kroc, the $75 Epilady did for the Krok sisters—Sharon, Arlene, and Loren.

In 1987 the three South African-born sisters acquired U.S. distribution rights to Epilady, a women's hair-removal device made in Israel. Epilady became one of the hottest products to hit the U.S. personal-care market in years. Sales hit $100 million their second year and are still climbing.

The most successful single product ever invented didn't do very much for the inventor, but the recognizer made a fortune. Dr. John Pemperton was a pharmacist in Atlanta when he concocted a new soft-drink formula in 1888. Two years later he sold out his interests in Coca-Cola for $1750.

The new owner was a wholesale druggist named Asa Candler. By 1903 Candler was a millionaire, and by 1914 his fortune had soared to $50 million. Two years later he was elected mayor of Atlanta. (After what Coca-Cola did for the city of Atlanta, it was the least that Atlanta could do for Asa Candler.)

When the Candler family sold The Coca-Cola Company to the Ernest Woodruff Group in 1919, the sale was the "largest business transaction ever consummated in the South."

Even the invention itself often turns out to be an accident. In 1850 Levi Strauss arrived in San Francisco with bolts of cloth to manufacture tents for miners in the year-old California Gold Rush.

That was a mistake, one Forty-Niner said. The thing prospectors needed the most were pants strong enough to withstand the rigors of the diggings.

So Strauss found his gold by cutting trousers instead of tents out of his tentcloth. (He used rivets on the pockets because that's the way you make tents.)

Today Levi's are the world's largest-selling brand of blue jeans and a fitting tribute to the flexibility of a tent maker named Strauss.

Across the Atlantic, Gustave Leven became as famous in France as Levi did here in the United States.

In early 1946 Mr. Leven's father, head of a family brokerage firm, asked him to find a buyer for a small spring in southern France that its British owner wanted to sell. The younger Mr. Leven contacted an old family friend, Samuel Bronfman, scion of the Seagram Corporation, to ask whether he wanted to add the spring to his beverage empire. Mr. Bronfman asked his friend to wait until autumn when he would come to France to visit the spring.

Mr. Leven didn't wait. He visited the famed bubbling spring in the town of Vergeze, whose springs have been known since the Roman times, and decided to buy the spring and its bottling operations, even though they were a shambles. He saw employees filling the small green bottles by plunging them into the spring by hand. Workers sometimes used their feet to put the bottle caps on.

The bottles, of course, were Perrier and they made Mr. Leven one of France's wealthiest men. He owns almost 20 percent of Source Perrier SA, which sells 4 billion bottles of water in 125 countries every year.

Be flexible. Too many single-minded, goal-oriented individuals remain fixated on tents when they could have made a fortune by shifting to trousers. Or they stick with a brokerage business when they could have made a bundle in bottled water.

The Idea Horse: 4 to 1

Everyone knows that an idea can take you to the top faster than anything else. But people sometimes expect too much of an idea. They want one that is not only great, but one that everyone else thinks is great too.

There are no such ideas. If you wait until an idea is ready to be accepted, it's too late. Someone else will have preempted it.

Or in the in/out vocabulary of a few years ago: Anything definitely in is already on its way out.

To ride the Idea Horse, you must be willing to expose yourself to ridicule and controversy. You must be willing to go against the tide.

You can't be first with a new idea unless you are willing to stick your neck out. And take a lot of abuse.

When Gustave Leven decided to launch Perrier in the United States, several consulting firms told him he would be foolish to try to sell sparkling water in the land of Coca-Cola drinkers. He ignored their advice.

(Even a little benzene in the bottles has failed to stop the flow of Perrier into the country.)

A good idea is seldom recognized as such. When Brian Epstein went to London to try to get a recording contract for the Beatles, he was snubbed. Among the rejections came the classic from Decca: "Go back to Liverpool, Mr. Epstein. Four-groups are out."

On the eve of the first Beatles tour of the United States, Jay Livingstone, head of Capitol Records, said, "We don't think the Beatles will do anything in this market."

Experts are usually wrong, especially when they pontificate on subjects which tend to reflect unfavorably on their own expertise. "Rock 'n' roll," said Frank Sinatra, "is phony and false and sung, written, and played for the most part by cretinous goons."

Photographer Richard Avedon once told Cher, "You will never make the cover of *Vogue* because you don't have blond hair or blue eyes." When she did, *Vogue* sold more copies than it had ever sold before.

A good idea has publicity value. And nothing has more publicity value than an idea that is shocking. Four clean-cut choir boys from Liverpool would have had a much harder time getting press than the Beatles did.

Advertising agencies have learned that shocking ads make good publicity. And good publicity makes a successful ad agency. Kirshenbaum & Bond is representative of the breed. "We needed to start hot. So we did the most outrageous advertising possible," says Jonathan Bond. Some examples:

- For Saint Laurie Ltd., a men's clothing store in New York: "Dress British. Think Yiddish."

- For Positano, a fashionable restaurant: "An authentic Italian restaurant where no one's been shot. Yet."

- For Hongson Importers' Jump sneakers, "The only way to get higher is illegal."

Perhaps the most shocking (for its time) and most famous advertisement was written 30 years ago by Shirley Polykoff for Miss Clairol hair color bath: "Does she ... or doesn't she?"

The ad became a legend and carried Ms. Polykoff right into the Advertising Copywriters' Hall of Fame.

The Other-Person Horse: 3 to 1

The key to your success is *always* somebody else. Even when you ride an idea or a product to the top, you are counting on others to recognize the value of the idea or the product.

You don't make a sale. Somebody else has to buy. What's true in selling products is also true in selling yourself. First somebody else has to recognize your good qualities and then "buy" you by giving you a job or a promotion.

In the course of a typical career, this selling and buying process takes place many times. Our surveys show that the average person needs to sell him- or herself seven times between the first big job and retirement. It can be a difficult and frustrating process.

Furthermore, the timing can be brutal. Let's say you were just fired. At the moment in your career when you need the most self-confidence, you now have the least. (How do you sell yourself if *you're* not sold on yourself?)

There is an easier way. One of the best horses to ride is the Other-Person Horse. You sell yourself once and the job is done.

At Capital Cities/ABC Inc., Daniel Burke climbed up the ladder behind Thomas Murphy. Murphy first met Burke, a fellow Harvard MBA, in 1955. (Keep in touch with people you meet who seem to be going somewhere, especially if you have something in common. People like to hire clones.)

When they met, Murphy was running a tiny television station in Albany, New York. It was operating out of a decaying nineteenth-century building that had been a home for nuns. Six years later, Murphy hired Burke away from General Foods to be his successor at the station, the first property of a company that would later be named Capital Cities.

Like Murphy before him, Daniel Burke moved from executive vice president to president and, when Murphy retired, to chairman and CEO.

The company wasn't standing still either. Along the way Cap Cities acquired TV and radio stations, magazines, newspapers, and the ABC network. What started with a single UHF outlet in Albany has become a media megamonster with some $5 billion in revenues.

It's not necessary to be a right-hand-man-or-woman type to ratchet your way up. You can be a specialist and still take advantage of levering someone else.

Mike Masterpool was a public relations officer working for Ross Johnson at Standard Brands. (The same Johnson who was later to play the leading role in the shootout at RJR Nabisco.)

When it came to spending money, the two were on the same wavelength. Masterpool, said Johnson admiringly, is "the only man who can take an unlimited budget and exceed it."

When Standard Brands merged with a much larger Nabisco, Johnson took over the reins and gave the public relations job to Masterpool. (The clones took over across the board. Within three years of the merger, 21 of the company's top 24 officers were Standard Brands people.)

The next merger was the big enchilada. Nabisco was bought by the much larger R. J. Reynolds. As soon as Johnson worked his way to the top, guess who he brought in as his public relations chief? Mike Masterpool, of course.

Finding a person to ride can be an easy way to the winner's circle. But at the same time it is probably the trickiest ride on the track.

Dan Quayle certainly rode to glory on the back of George Bush.

But a human horse, unlike a horse horse, has its own self-interest at heart. He or she will not blindly carry you where you want to go. They go where *they* want to go.

So when it's election time again, President Bush just might decide that young Dan could be a detriment to being reelected. (As Richard Nixon was nearly thrown out by Dwight Eisenhower.) If that's the case, Quayle will suddenly be horseless and categorized by the press as a political loser. That could be fatal to his political future.

So it is in Corporate America and the world at large. The person you're riding could find you expendable if you become a liability in any way.

The Partner Horse: 5 to 2

The Partner Horse, of course, is a variation of the Other-Person Horse. The difference is that partners are combinations of equals. Equality has a number of advantages. True partners trust each other. They can be objective with each other.

You're not a good judge of your own ideas. You need someone you can trust to evaluate your ideas, perhaps to suggest changes and modifications. And vice versa of course.

Partners can be a powerful combination in almost any business or professional situation. Two people can usually do better than either one would alone. Yet if you look around, you see mostly loners.

A loner often starts out well, with the advantage of youth, enthusiasm, energy, and a fresh approach. As you grow older, your ego grows along with your paycheck. You may gain some experience, but your inner talent rarely changes. As your ego begins to overwhelm your ability, you become a pompous know-it-all.

Your objectivity becomes smothered by your own pomposity. You become more and more critical of others. You fail to see merit in anybody's ideas except your own. Nobody can do a job the way you can do it. If your boss were a little brighter, he or she would see how capable you are and take all measures to promote you. Now you are really out of touch.

Most business people are out of touch. Your co-workers, remember, are your competitors. They see you as a competitor too. The rule of 99 percent states that only one out of 100 of you will make it up the ladder. Why should your coworkers give you a boost when it means that they will never get off the ground? Behind all those smiling faces in the morning are cunning minds looking for ways to exploit an advantage. No wonder everyone is a little paranoid.

A partner can keep you down to earth. A partner can supply the objectivity that will keep your ego in check. You'll be able to accomplish things together you wouldn't be able to do alone.

There's a long history of entrepreneurial partnerships in the business world. Jobs and Wozniak of Apple. Gates and Allen of Microsoft. But perhaps the most successful of all partnerships was the one that was started in 1938 by Bill Hewlett and Dave Packard, who launched their company in a garage behind a rooming house.

Today Hewlett-Packard is a $12 billion company with 95,000 employees and offices around the world.

In 1964 Phil Knight and Bill Bowerman got together to create a new kind of running shoe. The result was Nike, the world's largest athletic shoe company.

More recently Bruce Wasserstein and Joseph Perella walked away from First Boston Corp. to form a new mergers and acquisitions company. In their first year their new firm, Wasserstein Perella & Co., ranked an incredible second among merger advisors. Wasserstein Perella has been in on the biggest deals of recent years: Kraft, RJR Nabisco, Time Warner. To finance future growth, they sold 20 percent of the firm to Nomura Securities for $100 million, gaining capital and a Japanese connection in one shot.

The Spouse Horse: 2 to 1

How did Gilbert Grosvenor become the editor of the *National Geographic*? Was it his talent? Was it his love of travel? Or was it his love of Elsie May, the daughter of Alexander Graham Bell, the National Geographic Society president?

Grosvenor did a superb job. In his 55 years as editor, the membership of the society increased from less than a thousand to over 2 million.

Just as a flower needs a garden to grow in, talent needs an opportunity if it is going to flourish. Elsie May Bell was Gilbert Grosvenor's opportunity and he took it.

Ironically, Alexander Graham Bell's own father-in-law had founded the society a decade earlier.

History is loaded with stories of men and women who rode their spouses to success. Yet somehow it's not considered to be quite ethical. Most people would much rather make it on their own.

"I want to do it myself" seems to be the watchword of the younger set. (When you get older, you realize you might have missed a major opportunity.)

Our message is simple. *Everybody* needs a horse. Whether you find a stranger or a spouse shouldn't matter. The most important question to ask yourself is, "How good a horse is my spouse?"

Instead of reading the help-wanted classified ads in the morning, look across the breakfast table and ask, "Hey, dear, I was wondering if ...?"

A horse in the barn is worth two in the bush.

Melvin Gordon has been chairman and chief executive of Tootsie Roll Industries since 1962. He's done a superb job. Listed as one of *Forbes'* 200 best small companies, Tootsie Roll produces 18 million Tootsie Rolls a day. The company is booming with 12 straight years of record sales. In 1988 it reached $128 million.

Melvin Gordon and Gilbert Grosvenor have one thing in common: they both married the boss's daughter. There's a twist, however, in the story of the Tootsie tycoon.

After having four children, the daughter decided she wanted to have a career too. So she went to work for ... of course. Today Ellen Gordon is president of Tootsie Roll Industries.

"Hey, dear, I was wondering if ...?" Why not? What have you got to lose? And the odds for your success are a lot better than trying to ride a stranger.

Don't let your ego get in the way. Remember: Everybody needs a horse.

What's the downside of riding the Spouse Horse? The obvious thing that could go wrong is divorce.

Forty-five years ago, George Johnson founded a corporation which became the largest black-owned publicly traded company. His wife Joan became treasurer. He owned 49.5 percent of the Johnson Products Co. stock; she owned 6.8 percent. Then came the divorce.

As part of the settlement, George Johnson turned over his stock to his ex-wife and became a consultant to the company. Joan Johnson is now chairman. Their son Eric is now CEO. It seems like a wise decision on both sides.

Sometimes the boardroom ties are even stronger than the bedroom ties. Gale Hayman and her husband Fred Hayman created Giorgio, the Rodeo Drive boutique and the fragrance.

Giorgio was a fantastic success. It outsold every other fragrance introduced in the eighties.

Along the way the Haymans were divorced. But they continued to work together on their blockbuster phenomenon, Giorgio.

In 1987 the Haymans sold Giorgio to Avon for $165 million. Not a bad haul for a couple, married or divorced.

The Family Horse: 3 to 2

You can't divorce a son or daughter, or a parent for that matter. That fact alone gives this horse an advantage over the Spouse Horse.

The Family Horse is responsible for the many corporate dynasties you find in America today. Ford, Marriott, Busch, Bronfman, Tisch, Trump. The list is longer than you might think.

One hundred and seventy-five of the *Fortune* 500 largest industrial companies are family controlled, according to *Family Business* magazine. That's 35 percent. (The magazine defines family control as 25 percent ownership with at least two family members involved in running the company.)

That definition leaves out some big companies with large family ownership positions. For example, 59 percent of Campbell Soup is owned by the Dorrance family, all descendants of the condensed-soup inventor

John T. Dorrance. (The three children of the late John
T. Dorrance Jr. control 32 percent of the stock, while 27
percent is spread among six other family groups.) Yet
Campbell is not considered a family business because
no one in the Dorrance family works at the company.

What a wasted opportunity. Let's say you were part
of the Dorrance family. The thing to do is to approach
Campbell and say, "Hey, board of directors, I was wondering if ...?"

By way of contrast, consider the Jervis B. Webb Co.,
a worldwide enterprise engaged in engineering, fabricating, and installing materials-handling equipment.
Sales are more than $300 million a year.

Fourteen top management jobs are held by descendants of the original Jervis B. Webb or their spouses,
including the current chairman Jervis C. Webb and his
younger brother George H., who is president. Both
Webbs are sons of the founder.

Even at Ford Motor Co., the Ford name lives on. Although Henry Ford II died in 1987, there are still four
Fords, including Edsel Ford and William Clay Ford Jr.,
active in the company.

At Ford and at other family-controlled businesses,
you find the theory of relativity is at work. You do better if the name on your door matches the name on the
building.

What's true in business (Ford) is true in politics
(Kennedy). It's also true in the movies. Consider these
names: Fonda (Henry, Jane, Peter), Huston (Walter,
John, Anjelica), Bridges (Lloyd, Beau, Jeff), and
Carradine (John, David, Keith, Robert).

Then there's Kirk Douglas and son. With an Academy Award for the movie *Wall Street* and juicy roles in *Fatal Attraction* and *Romancing the Stone,* Michael Douglas has become an even bigger star than his old man.

When Kirk Douglas accepted an award from the people in his hometown in upstate New York, he made a little speech with his son in the audience. "It was a lot easier for me to become successful than it was for my son. Michael made it despite having a famous father. And that takes some doing."

In polite company this is known as "el toro poo-poo."

6

The Company Horse

In a previous chapter, we put the Company Horse in the long-shot category and quoted the odds at 50 to 1. But companies vary and so do the odds.

The general principle? The larger the company, the higher the odds; the smaller the company, the lower the odds. Yet the paradox is that most people want to work for big companies because they perceive that's where the most opportunities are.

First of all, the mathematics are against you. Take the *Fortune* 500, the cream of the corporate crop. These 500 largest U.S. industrial companies employ some 12 million people—about 10 percent of the total civilian population of 118 million employees. Chances are only one in ten that a given person will wind up working for a *Fortune* 500 company.

Nor do the odds change much in light of where you went to school. Again, the perception is that the business schools turn out MBAs primarily for the big companies. The reality is quite different. Take the Harvard Business School, the West Point of the corporate world.

An analysis of the class of 1970, in the prime of their business careers, shows that only 10 percent work for companies that employ 25,000 or more employees. (Thirty-six percent are self-employed.)

These are not unsuccessful people. Most of them are wealthy; 56 percent are millionaires. Many earn substantial salaries; 34 percent have annual incomes of $250,000 or more. Most of them, however, do not work for big companies.

The ones that do wind up with the giant corporations find the pathway to the top daunting. It's what Judith Barwick, author of *The Plateauing Trap,* calls "The Rule of 99 Percent." To wit: "Of one hundred people who are hired because they have all the right qualities and look outstanding, only ten will reach any level of middle management and only one will reach the executive level."

With odds like these, who would want to get into the game? Surprisingly, a lot of people want to. (The *Fortune* 500 turn down a lot more executive candidates than they hire.) But after you are on board, what are your chances for moving up?

The brutal truth is that ability is one of the least important attributes for success. Corporations aren't rational entities that unfailingly do what is best for the individual. Corporations are collections of people or egos who are trying to get ahead of their running mates.

In many ways, they resemble races like the New York Marathon. Thousands of people are off at the gun, jostling and elbowing each other for position. The early turns are vicious, with no holds barred. It's not until the race has been run for a while that the pack thins out and you get some running room.

There are five ways to the top of the corporate jungle gym. None are easy. All are difficult.

1. Be an Early Bird

When you read the biographies of many CEOs, you might be surprised to learn how many joined their companies very early in the corporate life cycle. Some were directly involved in the formation of the company. Others were among their companies' first employees.

In 1956 Fred Turner dropped out of Drake University to work as a counterman in Ray Kroc's first McDonald's restaurant in Des Plaines, Illinois. Later that year he became a $100-a-week assistant manager at Kroc's second restaurant.

The Early Bird catches the eye of the founder. Seventeen years later, Ray Kroc named Fred Turner chief executive officer of McDonald's.

In 1967 Joe Lee dropped out of Valdosta State College to work for Bill Darden, owner of Darden's Green Frog, a popular South Georgia restaurant.

Darden shared with Lee his dream of opening low-priced, family-oriented seafood restaurants. Lee, along with two others, helped Darden develop the first unit in Lakeland, Florida. Instead of the Green Frog, they called it the Red Lobster. Joe Lee was the restaurant's first manager.

Five units later, Darden sold the chain to General Mills. Today Joe Lee is president of General Mills Restaurants, a group which includes 550 Red Lobster seafood restaurants and 170 Olive Garden Italian dinner houses. Together they have sales of well over a billion dollars.

Wendy's International was a two-unit chain when

Robert L. Barney joined the organization in 1971. Nine years later, he was named chief executive officer, succeeding Wendy's founder, R. David Thomas. When Barney retired in 1990, Wendy's was a 3800-unit chain doing $1.1 billion in sales.

Another Early Bird in the fast food field was John Young Brown, Jr. Brown was a 29-year-old lawyer when he first met Colonel Harland Sanders in 1963.

The following year, Brown and a partner, Jack Massey, bought the Colonel's company for $2 million. (Half a million down and the remainder over a five-year period.) The company they bought from Colonel Sanders, of course, was Kentucky Fried Chicken. Massey supplied the money (with a little help from the Third National Bank of Nashville) and Brown supplied the management talent.

Seven years later Brown and Massey sold Kentucky Fried Chicken to Heublein for $285 million. Brown's share was $35 million. Not bad for seven years of work and no financial investment.

In 1979 John Young Brown, Jr., married Phyllis George (Miss America 1971). After a brief honeymoon, he announced that "we have decided" to run for governor of Kentucky.

How could he lose, with Kentucky Fried Chicken on one wing and Phyllis George on the other? He won in a landslide.

It might be worth noting that the Browns were married by Norman Vincent Peale. It wouldn't surprise us to find that John Brown credits his success to positive thinking.

Think positive if you will, but at the same time go out and find your own Colonel Harland Sanders.

C. R. Smith was a 29-year-old bookkeeper at the Texas-Louisiana Power Co. when he was offered the job of treasurer at a small airmail carrier. Called Texas Air Transport, the company eventually became American Airlines and C. R. Smith became one of its first chief executives, a job he held, off and on, for 32 years. Along the way, he became a legend in the airline industry and undoubtedly its most famous executive.

When he was first offered the Texas Air job, Smith said, "I have no interest in aviation." How could he have had any interest in aviation when there was practically no aviation industry to be interested in. Fortunately for Smith, he took the job anyway.

The best time to ride the Company Horse is early. And the best Company Horse to ride is the leader in a leading-edge industry. How do you recognize a leading-edge industry? It's a lot easier after the fact. Aviation in the thirties. Radio in the forties. Television in the fifties. The personal computer in the eighties.

Opportunities occur not just at the top of a leading-edge company, but up and down the ladder. Carol Bartz got her ticket punched at a big company (Digital Equipment Corp.) and then joined Sun Microsystems in 1983 when it was still a fledgling. Bartz built Sun's marketing department from 10 people to a staff of 120. In 1987 she took over Sun's federal division and tripled government sales to $115 million in just a year. As a reward, she was promoted to vice president for worldwide field operations, and she still has a long career ahead of her. Carol Bartz is only 41.

The personal computer was the leading-edge industry of the eighties. What will become the next leading-edge industry? No one knows until after the fact. That makes riding the Company Horse a big gamble, which is why we assigned such big odds to this venture.

What you can do, however, to increase your own personal odds is to cross off your prospect list all the companies that are definitely not leading-edge candidates. These include virtually all the giant corporations: the General Motors, General Electrics, and General Dynamics of this world. As a matter of fact, cross off any company starting with the word General, Standard, International, or American.

If you insist on trying your luck at a company that's already big, you need a different strategy from the Early Bird strategy. Let's move on to a second approach.

2. Be a Politician

Ross Perot was once asked by Tom Watson how successful he would have been if he had stayed at IBM. "I'd be somewhere in middle management, being asked to take early retirement," said Perot. "I would not have been successful in a big corporation. I'm too direct. Too purposeful."

Life in a big company is a bowl of spaghetti. You can't be too direct. You have to be indirect. You have to learn how to be a politician.

You can't work your way to the top of a company. You have to be "promoted."

Who does the promoting? Other people. That's why to get ahead at a big company, you have to become a Politician. Doing a good job is only the first step. You have to find a way to let others know you are doing a good job. Your job skills are secondary to your political skills.

If you unwrap the life history of any successful executive, you will usually find the name of one or more "sponsors."

When Thomas invited Barney to join Wendy's, he wasn't talking to a stranger. The two had worked together selling Kentucky Fried Chicken.

If you want to get ahead at a big company, work hard and keep your nose clean. But that only buys you a lottery ticket. To claim one of the big prizes, you're going to need a sponsor.

Let's differentiate between a mentor and a sponsor. A mentor is someone, usually older than you are, who takes a personal interest in your career and winds up giving you free advice.

A sponsor will also take a personal interest in your career and give you free advice, but he or she will go one step further. A sponsor will promote you or, at the very least, will use his or her influence with others who can promote you.

If you work for one of the *Fortune* 500 companies or a big institution of any kind, the first and most important question to ask yourself is not "How am I doing?" It's "Who is my sponsor?" Without a sponsor, you'll never go anywhere.

It doesn't matter how good a job you are doing. Many big companies are notorious for taking good people who are doing a good job and leaving them exactly where they are. (Why take a chance on promoting somebody to a different position only to wind up with two jobs being done poorly?)

Don't big companies move people around to give

them a broader experience? Sure they do. These are the young people with sponsors.

Many companies maintain carefully hidden lists of "high potential" employees. Are you on your company's fast-track list? Find out as soon as you can. It might save you years of heartbreak. If you're not on the list, our suggestion is to read on and move on. You can't push a string up a hill. It has to be pulled up.

When Walter Wriston was Citicorp CEO, the bank had 2437 places of business in 95 countries with 59,000 people on the employee list.

The list that really counted, however, had only 75 names. It was called the Corporate Property List, and it contained the names of the 75 people who were thought to have top management potential.

Citicorp's personnel department scheduled visits for Wriston to see some of these lower-level people around the organization. What did he talk about? Families, sports, hobbies, and activities outside the business.

You can see the pattern. If you want to get ahead in a big corporation, you have to be a Politician. You have to make friends and not waves. In the corporate environment, words speak louder than actions. Especially if the words are spoken to the right people at the right time. By all means, tell the chief executive about your spouse and fine kids, the religious group you belong to, the Boy or Girl Scout troop that meets in your home, and the many charities you support with your time and money.

Don't be controversial. Don't be pro-abortion. Don't be anti-abortion. Especially don't take unpopular positions on such issues as the legalization of drugs. Let the *retired* politicians like former Secretary of State George Shultz do that.

What is a Politician except a mirror that reflects the interests and ideas of his or her constituents? When a Politician doesn't play back the right message, the voters break the mirror.

"People like people who are like themselves," said Wriston. "That's why clones are so popular." He said it to warn his people against falling into the clone trap.

Look at the top management of Citicorp today and what do you see? White male clones.

Or take Goldman, Sachs & Company, the largest private partnership on Wall Street. Goldman, Sachs has 128 partners. One woman and 127 men.

Nor is the gender balance likely to change in the short term. When asked about adding a second woman, a Goldman, Sachs partner said, "We do not have anyone who looks like a serious partner candidate in the near future." Of course, a woman doesn't *look like* a man.

When you work for a big company, you have two choices: (1) get on a fast-track list, or (2) get out of the company.

Just because you have a title doesn't mean you're on the list. Sometimes big companies hand out titles "in lieu of." In lieu of money, in lieu of a promotion, in lieu of a bigger office, etc.

Ogilvy & Mather, the advertising agency, has 320 vice presidents or better. Not all of these vice and senior vice presidents are going on to bigger and better things. Most are not. As a percentage of total employees, Ogilvy & Mather has 20 percent who are ranked vice president and above. DDB Needham has 19 percent. McCann Erickson and Young & Rubican have 16 percent vice presidents and above.

"And above" is a pretty big category all by itself. Try calling Saatchi & Saatchi in New York and asking for the chairman. "Which one?" is the receptionist's reply. Saatchi & Saatchi has three chairmen, two presidents, three vice chairmen, two chief operating officers, and a slew of executive and senior vice presidents.

Banking is even worse. Being the vice president of a bank usually means you have a desk to sit at. Citibank has thousands of vice presidents and so does Chase Manhattan.

At one point in time, the investment banking firm of Wasserstein, Perella & Company had a chairman, an international chairman, four vice chairmen, 17 managing directors, and 15 vice presidents. All to manage some 100 professionals.

Being a clone, finding a sponsor, and getting on the fast-track list are the three most important attributes of a Politician. The rise of Roger Smith at General Motors illustrates all three.

The three previous chairmen (Fred Donner, Richard Gerstenberg, and Tom Murphy) had all been accountants. Smith was an accountant.

In the mid-fifties, Murphy was a General Motors financial analyst in charge of preparing facts and figures for critical antitrust hearings in Washington, D.C. Smith was asked to help.

Smith helped Murphy prepare numerous studies, filled with facts and figures demonstrating General Motors' positive effect on the nation's employment and the gross national product. The hearings were a success and Smith had a sponsor.

As Murphy moved up, he pulled Smith along with him. In 1974 Tom Murphy became chairman. Smith was named executive vice president of finance. Six years later, Smith moved into the driver's seat.

Our studies reveal one striking characteristic of the big corporation. No one on the inside makes it to the top without a *personal* relationship with the previous CEO. Sometimes these relationships go on for decades, long before the previous CEO first assumed the top job.

That's the advantage of a staff position like finance. It gives you a personal, sometimes day-to-day exposure to the CEO. If you're in a line position out in the sticks, you may not see the CEO for months at a time. This gives the political types in the staff jobs at headquarters endless opportunities to bad-mouth you.

You also have to be schizophrenic to ride the Company Horse. You have to be a team player on the outside but a rugged individualist on the inside. You have to sugar-coat your competitive instincts.

"A high proportion of people who get to the top are conflict avoiders," observes Dee Soder, an executive counselor on psychological matters. "They don't like hearing negatives. They don't like saying or thinking negative things. They frequently make it up the ladder in part because they don't irritate people on the way up."

The bigger the company, the more likely it is that all the nonteam players will be weeded out long before the top layers are reached. When you work for a big company like General Motors, you have to constantly demonstrate your loyalty, not your intelligence.

It's the difference between a cat and a dog. A dog will wag its tail to welcome you home. A dog will fawn over you and be responsive to your every whim. A cat, on the other hand, will generally ignore you and be in-different to your wishes. A cat has its own priorities.

Corporations have a lot of cats and dogs working for them. The dogs are eager, enthusiastic, good-natured, clumsy team players. The cats are quiet, competent, thoughtful, even-tempered individualists.

So who gets promoted? The dogs, of course, Who is smarter? It's a scientific fact that cats are a lot smarter than dogs. If you want to get to the top, be smart like a cat and act like a dog.

Maybe that's not the way it ought to be. Maybe com-panies would be a lot better off if they ignored the dogs and paid more attention to the cats. But surely that's the way it is. If you want to ride the Company Horse, you have to pay the price.

One of the smartest cats in the automobile business is Jim La Marre. He was the marketing genius behind the rise of Volvo, which has become the largest-selling European luxury car in the U.S. market. But he is also a proud and stubborn man.

To get along in the corporate world, you have to compromise your principles. After Volvo in Sweden ap-proved the company's participation in a Washington, D.C., exhibition sponsored by the U.S. Department of Transportation, La Marre in New Jersey said no. It was a matter of principle to Volvo's resident marketing ge-nius, who shortly thereafter left the company.

Those who challenge the system, the way La Marre tried to do, are branded as not good team players. If they are not forced out of the company, they usually find their road to the top permanently blocked. Whistle blowers beware. When you work for a corporate behemoth, the subliminal message is: you join the team or you join the unemployed.

On his first day in office as the new chairman of General Motors, Robert Stempel held a press conference. The purpose of the meeting was to introduce the Stempel "team," the seven top GM executives (all men, of course) who would run the company in the twenty-first century. During short remarks by Mr. Stempel and other executives the words *team* or *teamwork* were used 24 times. Presumably these are members of the same team who introduced losers like Fiero, Cimarron, and Allanté.

Teamwork is not the exclusive property of the big corporations. Many small companies also worship the concept. And they can be hard on people who deviate from official policy.

Andreas Bechtolsheim is one of the founders of Sun Microsystems, the largest manufacturer of computer workstations. While still a student at Stanford, the West German native designed his first computer, a so-called workstation for engineers and scientists. When he couldn't sell the machine to a large computer company (the not-invented-here problem), Mr. Bechtolsheim founded Sun in 1982 with three partners. In spite of Sun's spectacular success, all is not sweetness and light. When Bechtolsheim proposed building the Sparc-station, a desk-top workstation, Sun's senior executives objected. He came close to quitting and setting up his own company.

As a matter of fact, Bechtolsheim did form a new company called UniSun to bring his new computer to market. The dispute was settled when Sun agreed to build the Sparcstation and Bechtolsheim sold UniSun back to Sun. As you might have expected, Sparcstation was a big success. Today it accounts for about 75 percent of unit sales of all Sun computers.

3. Be a Flasher

If you want to get ahead, you have to find a way to expose yourself to top management. It works in big business and it also works in big government.

Stephen Potts is a Washington lawyer who was appointed to the nation's top ethics post in June 1990. Although chosen to head the Office of Government Ethics, Mr. Potts had no background in either government or ethics law, and he had not worked in the Bush campaign. How did he meet the President, Mr. Potts was asked.

On the tennis court, he replied. Nor is he alone in this respect.

Nicholas Brady, now Treasury Secretary, first met George Bush on the tennis court.

James Baker, now Secretary of State, became friends with George Bush when the two won the doubles championship at the Houston Country Club.

Roger Porter, domestic policy chief, first met George Bush when President Ford invited the two to the White House for a doubles match.

David Bates, former Cabinet secretary, played tennis as a boy with Bush's son Jeb.

Tennis is only one way to the top of a big organization. The initial ingredient is exposure. If you can't find a way to expose yourself to top management, you're out of luck. If you've worked for General Electric for 20 years and Jack Welch doesn't know you personally, you're not going to go anywhere at GE.

The personal connection is the key to working your way up the corporate ladder. In a study of the Harvard Business School class of 1949, *Fortune* magazine said, "Hardly anyone who made it big did so without a leg up from someone."

Celebrated as "the class the dollars fell on," this group is famous for the CEOs it produced and the wealth it amassed. Tom Murphy, chief executive of Capital Cities/ABC, was taken in by Frank Smith, a friend of Murphy's father and founder of Cap Cities. When Smith died in 1966, Murphy succeeded him at the age of 41.

James Burke, until recently chief executive of Johnson & Johnson, made friends as a young man with Bobby Johnson, son of the company's CEO. The friendship gave him a big boost up the corporate ladder.

IBM's Tom Watson, Sr., was noted for taking an instant liking to someone and promoting him. Once, when he was listening to a presentation by one of IBM's youngest branch managers, he said impulsively, "That man on the platform is so impressive that he will be our new general sales manager. I am going to make the announcement right now." And he did, to the consternation of the audience, because the man on the platform went from a junior position to practically everyone's boss.

The power of a personal connection can also be seen in the rise of Watson's secretaries. Fred Nichol was Watson's secretary at National Cash Register and moved with him to IBM. Eventually Nichol was promoted to vice president and general manager, the No. 2 position at IBM. John Phillips also started as Watson's secretary and eventually rose to president and vice chairman of the board of IBM. If you want to get ahead, get close to the source of power.

John Opel was an administrative assistant to Tom Watson, Jr. Opel eventually became chairman, another in a long line of IBM people to profit from a personal connection at the top.

Outside professionals and management consultants have plenty of opportunities to make personal connections with top management. Many consultants have moved directly from McKinsey, Booz-Allen, or Bain to top spots in client organizations. A consultant has two advantages over an employee when both are being considered for the same high-level job:

1. The consultant has greater stature. (The client treats the consultant as an equal, not as an underling.)

2. The consultant is smarter. (Anybody who charges hundreds of dollars an hour must know a thing or two.)

Lawyers have often demonstrated the power of the pure personal connection. With no experience managing people and little knowledge of the products and markets involved, many lawyers have managed to get themselves hired to run major corporations. There's something about the client-lawyer relationship that puts the lawyer on a pedestal. In the boardroom a lawyer seems to know exactly how the law will interpret every issue. (In the courtroom, there are a lot more differences of opinion.)

Richard Donahue was recently named president and chief operating officer of Nike Inc., the $2 billion athletic shoe company. A partner in Donahue and Donahue, a family law firm in Lowell, Massachusetts, Mr. Donahue had been a Nike director for 12 years. Yet he had limited experience in running a company and limited experience in the shoe industry. What he did have is a close friendship with Phil Knight, Nike's CEO and founder.

Such stories are the tip of the iceberg. It's not just lawyers and consultants who parlay a personal connection to the top. The truth is, most executives who made the long climb up the ladder did so by virtue of a personal connection. Buried in the memories of thousands of presidents and chairmen are the real reasons for their rise to the top. The presentation, the board meeting, the luncheon, the golf game. Chances are, there was an occasion where the young CEO-to-be caught the attention of someone at the top. From that moment on, he or she was a marked person.

If you want to get into the running for the top, you first have to get the attention of the people who are already there. It's not easy. General Electric has more than 292,000 employees. How many of those people do you suppose Jack Welch knows by name? We'd guess about 400. (And he probably has negative thoughts about 350 of the employees he does know.)

If you work for GE, your problem is not your job, your salary, or even your latest performance review. Your problem is visibility. How do you get noticed by Jack?

Don't do something stupid like writing him a letter, explaining your thoughts about a new corporate strategy for General Electric. That's instant death. And you never get a second chance to make a first impression.

Actually, depending upon your position, you have to work your way up the visibility ladder. Your boss knows you and your boss's boss probably does too. But how about the person who occupies the third rung above you? How do you catch this person's attention?

Absolutely the best way is the same way that got the general sales manager's job for the young IBM branch manager. Make an outstanding presentation.

To have a chance to sit in the chairman's chair, you have to be good on your feet. No talent will take you as far as the ability to make a good presentation. The ability to speak well is more important to your future success than the ability to think or the ability to write. The mouth is more powerful than the mind. (You can always tap the thinking of those around you. And one of the advantages of working in a big company is that there are always a lot of people around you.)

If you're still in school, take as many public speaking courses as you can. If you've left the halls of ivy, put as much effort into your company presentations as you possibly can. You never know when someone from top management will just happen to drop in while you're speaking.

And above all, practice, practice, practice. Speech is like golf. No matter how much natural talent you have, you'll do better if you practice. And if you can get a tape of one of your presentations, listen, listen, listen. You won't like everything you hear, but it will help you perfect your speaking style. (A miniature recorder to tape your presentations and speeches can do more to advance your corporate career than a personal computer.)

4. Be a Hero

This can be tricky. You have to become famous on the inside while at the same time you remain almost invisible on the outside.

How do you become a Hero inside your own company? The simplest, most direct way is to attach yourself to the most visible, most exciting new product or service your company is planning to introduce.

Robert Shapiro spent 16 years as a lawyer before joining G. D. Searle in 1979. Because of their trademark and patent experience, lawyers often have the inside track when it comes to a new product assignment. Shapiro's big break came when he was assigned to the NutraSweet group, first as president and then, after Searle was bought by Monsanto, as chairman. Thanks to a strong patent position and the phenomenal success of diet products, NutraSweet made a fortune for Monsanto ($180 million in 1989 on sales of $869 million, even after a bookkeeping charge of $180 million related to patent values).

Shapiro's reward was a promotion to Monsanto's big agricultural-products business. As the new president of Monsanto Agricultural Co., Mr. Shapiro is now in line for the top job. (You can't be CEO of Monsanto without one foot on the farm. Roundup and other crop chemicals are twice as big as NutraSweet.)

Making yourself visible at Monsanto is one thing, but how do you do it at General Motors, the world's largest company? GM has 775,000 employees world-wide, including 36 vice presidents, but aside from Robert Stempel, the person who has the most visible assignment is Skip LeFauve.

LeFauve is president of Saturn Corp. "More than a car," says *Business Week*, "it is GM's hope for reinventing itself." When Saturn was formed as an independent subsidiary, then chairman Roger Smith proclaimed it "the key to GM's long-term competitiveness, survival, and success." If the sun shines on Saturn, is there any doubt that LeFauve will follow Stempel into the chairman's chair?

Aside from making sure Saturn is a success (a difficult task indeed), LeFauve has only one potential problem: personal publicity. Too much and he's dead meat. Those 36 vice presidents will have him for lunch.

The tendency in big companies today is to sit back and play it safe. Don't get trapped into taking a high-profile Saturn-type job. Sometimes it works; sometimes it doesn't. It depends upon what your competitors do. If one of them scores big in a high-visibility assignment, you could sit back, play it safe, and lose out.

The same principle applies if you do get one of those big-ticket assignments. The tendency is to approach the job cautiously, feeling your way around for a couple of months until you get both feet on the ground. That's a mistake. Make sure you take strong, bold actions as soon as possible.

For the first 100 days, you are bullet-proof. Make sure you do the right things the right way, especially the nasty ones like shutting down a plant or product line or firing employees. The person who put you in the job can't fire you in the first couple of months. It would reflect unfavorably on that person. You have a free hand. Use it.

The opposite of a high-visibility assignment is a position that provides "good experience." An overseas assignment, for example. Avoid these. Take no job that's out of the line of sight of the chief executive. These assignments are dead ends. You can't win even if you're a winner.

In a truly big company like General Motors, at least 98 percent of all executive jobs are dead ends. They never lead anywhere because they don't have the respect of top management or because the jobs are not in management's line of sight. Take an advertising or public relations position, for example. You will never go anywhere from one of these jobs at GM. Get another assignment or get out.

There are hundreds of similar jobs in major corporations. They have never led anywhere and they never will. Don't try to fight the system. And don't let someone tell you jobs like these are "good experience." They are good experience, but only in a negative way. "Now I know why I never should have taken that job" is the only experience you'll get.

When a company is doing well, it tends to promote from the inside. That's when the Politician or the Hero takes over. But when a company is doing poorly, the insider doesn't have a chance. New blood is required.

Things can get really bad. Look at Chrysler in 1978 or Western Union today. When a company is "down," it's a Catch 22 situation. "If you're stupid enough to work for us, you can't seriously believe we would select you as our chief executive."

5. Be a White Knight

Lee Iacocca arrived at Chrysler on a white horse, fresh from his successes at Ford. That's not unusual.

When a big company gets into trouble, it often turns to the CEO of a more successful competitor. Chrysler was lucky to find Iacocca available. Iacocca was an exception because he moved from a bigger company to a smaller one. Most of the moves are in the other direction, from smaller to bigger.

If you play your cards right, you can White Knight your way to the top in a hurry.

At the age of 46, Stephen M. Wolf became chairman and president of Allegis Corp. His first move was to change the name back to UAL Corporation, the holding company for United Airlines.

How do you get to be chairman of an airline with 63,000 employees at the relatively young age of 46? You don't work your way up the Allegis ladder. Allegis was a broken ladder.

Actually, the airline had a hotshot by the name of John Zeeman who, by all odds, should have had Wolf's job. But everybody at United got tarred by the Allegis disaster.

"Our name may not mean a lot now, but will mean a lot in the future," said Richard J. Ferris, the previous chairman. "Allegis will be the umbrella for the expectations we want our customers to have when they fly United, rent a Hertz car, or stay at a Westin or Hilton International hotel."

After Ferris resigned, the Allegis board turned to White Knight Wolf. Insiders didn't make the cut. (They should have stopped Ferris from doing something foolish.)

Wolf has had a lot of White Knight experience. He spent his early years at American Airlines becoming a divisional vice president. His first White Knight move was to Continental as president in 1982, departing just before Frank Lorenzo put the carrier into bankruptcy. Wolf rode over to Republic Airlines and then to Flying Tigers.

From American to Continental to Republic to Flying Tigers to United: the route to the top in the airline industry is often marked by frequent flight changes.

White Knights are industry's version of free-agent baseball players. It took a $6 million employment package to lure Wolf from Tiger International Inc. (For that kind of money, they could have had Daryl Strawberry.)

White Knights are not always men, especially in industries such as retailing, fashion, and cosmetics.

At the age of 37, Robin Burns became president and chief executive of Estée Lauder USA, the cosmetic company's biggest division, with sales of $650 million. In addition to Estée Lauder, the best-selling department store cosmetic brand, the company also markets Clinique for women and the Aramis line for men.

Robin Burns' cosmetic career started at Bloomingdale's. In 1983 she joined Minnetonka as president of the company's Calvin Klein division. (Minnetonka founder Robert R. Taylor says he hired her after watching her take charge in a meeting that included top Bloomingdale executives.)

Calvin Klein wasn't much of a company ($6 million in annual sales) until Robin Burns, together with the designer, launched the hit fragrance Obsession. Sales soared to more than $200 million in 1989, and Ms. Burns was ready for her next challenge.

The White Knight market promises to get bigger as big companies run into trouble. As a matter of fact, three of the four largest U.S. industrial companies have run into serious difficulties. General Motors, Exxon, and IBM. (The fourth company is Ford, so far in good shape.)

When companies get into trouble, they turn to White Knights. "Hiring outside managers," said Richard M. Ferry of Korn Ferry International, the largest management recruiting firm, "is expected to be a leading trend of the nineties."

To sum up, the Company Horse is the most popular horse in America to ride. Each year, millions of college graduates flock to interview with the corporate recruiters. "The bigger, the better" seems to be the rule when deciding which job offer to take.

Be forewarned. Unless you have the foresight to be an Early Bird, the stomach to be a Politician, the fortitude to be a Flasher, or the luck to be a Hero or a White Knight, the road to the top will be difficult.

A company, especially a big and prestigious company, is a good place to get your ticket punched. With an IBM or a GE on your résumé, you may be able to parlay the experience to get a ride on a better horse.

And when you leave the big company, don't burn your bridges behind you. Just say "Goodbye, good luck, and I'll keep in touch." You'll find you can use those corporate friends as you change horses for the drive down the stretch.

7

The Product Horse

"I'd never be able to dream up an idea for a new product. That's not what I'm good at." Is that what you're thinking?

If so, don't skip this chapter. Whether you're creative or not doesn't make any difference. You can ride the Product Horse without having an ounce of creative talent.

Actually talent can get in your way. It's the ability to *recognize* the talent of others that's the key to making a fortune betting on the Product Horse.

Chester Carlson made a few bucks by inventing, but the management at Haloid made many large fortunes by recognizing the value of Carlson's invention.

Almost every major product breakthrough has a cast of at least two characters. On one half of the stage is the inventor. On the other half is the recognizer.

The inventors may get the top billing, but the recognizers get the top bucks. Dick and Mac McDonald versus Ray Kroc and associates, for example.

Even the inventor is often
a recognizer

An inventor is frequently pictured as someone who sits around saying, "I'd like to be a millionaire. Let's see, what can I invent?"

That picture doesn't square with reality. Most inventions, if not accidents, are heavily dependent on recognizing something happening outside yourself.

When Chester Carlson graduated from college with a degree in physics, Chester Carlson couldn't get work as a physicist. (*Accident No. 1.*)

Eventually he landed in the New York City patent office of a small electronics company assembling patent applications. (*Accident No. 2.*)

The job required making copies of drawings and specifications, a task Carlson found tedious and boring. Frustration was the spark that lit the fire of xerography. Carlson decided to invent a simpler method of copying. (*Think negative, not positive.*)

His next step was not to rush into a laboratory and whip up a bunch of chemicals. Why invent something that had already been invented? He studied everything written on photography and the physics of light. After months of paper research, he discovered a property known as photoconductivity, the manner in which light affects the electrical conductivity of materials. That key insight ultimately led to the xerography invention.

Get outside of yourself. Let your genius be more a matter of seeing what's happening on the outside than of inventing something in the vacuum of your mind. An inventor needs a horse to ride. Even a moldy horse will sometimes do.

Take the case of Alexander Fleming. The accident took the form of a stray penicillium mold which landed on a bacteria-filled petri dish in Fleming's laboratory. About to discard the dish, Fleming noticed that the mold had dissolved the bacterial colonies. That was the recognizer step.

From there it was only a matter of time before the introduction of penicillin, the first antibiotic.

Many financially successful inventions have been based on simple observations. Ann Moore was a Peace Corps volunteer in Africa when she noticed local women carrying their babies in slings of folded material. In 1984 she patented a soft, comfortable infant carrier that parents could strap to their backs or chests.

That observation became the Snugli, now almost standard equipment for new parents.

Beware of market research

After you find a good-looking Product Horse, your first inclination might be to take it to a vet and have it checked out. In other words, do a little market research.

Be careful. The big product ideas don't usually test out very well. For example, Univac pioneered a big product idea called the computer, only to lose its early lead to IBM. One reason Univac lost out was its own market research which confidently predicted that by the year 2000 there would be only 1000 computers in use. Why invest in a product with such a limited potential market?

Unfortunately for Univac, IBM didn't spend the money on research, so they didn't learn the bad news about computers. Instead they geared up for a market that proceeded to exceed every market researcher's wildest dreams.

Unfortunately for IBM, IBM did spend money to research the plain-paper copier. In 1959 Haloid approached IBM to complete the development of the 914 and handle its introduction.

IBM hired a consulting firm, Arthur D. Little, to study the copier market and advise it on how to respond to Haloid's request for help. On the basis of extensive financial and market analysis, Arthur D. Little projected that no more than 5000 of the new Xerox machines would sell. (That was 5000 in total.)

Naturally, IBM declined to help. Eight years later, Xerox (the new name for the Haloid Company) had manufactured and placed 190,000 copiers. Total employment at Xerox had jumped from 900 to more than 24,000.

Whether you work for a big company or a small one, whether you work for yourself or someone else, sooner or later you will run across a 914 in the row. Will you recognize it when you see it?

Paul Allen and Bill Gates were Seattle high school buddies who wound up in Massachusetts. Allen was working for Honeywell. Gates was a freshman at Harvard.

Walking through Harvard Square one day, Allen noticed the cover of the January 1975 issue of *Popular Electronics*. "PROJECT BREAKTHROUGH! World's First Minicomputer Kit to Rival Commercial Models ... ALTAIR 8800."

Allen ran to tell Gates that their big break had come. They knew how to write computer software. They would write a basic software program for the Altair 8800, the world's first personal computer.

Six weeks later Allen flew to Albuquerque, home of MITS, Inc., makers of the Altair 8800. The demonstration was successful and Microsoft made its first sale as a microcomputer software house. Allen was 20 years old. Gates was 19.

Paul Allen, who left Microsoft in 1983 to fight Hodgkin's disease (successfully), still owns $1 billion in stock. Bill Gates owns more than $2 billion.

Timing in life is extremely important. (More on this later.) Where would Microsoft be today if Gates and Allen had not seen that *Popular Electronics* cover, if they had not called MITS owner Ed Roberts, if Allen had not flown to Albuquerque?

What were you doing in 1975? Did you see the Altair computer story in *Popular Electronics*? Did you send in your $397 check to buy one?

Two thousand people did. Harry Garland, one of the magazine's contributors, said in awe: "It was an absolute, runaway, overnight, insane success."

Aside from Allen and Gates, Jobs and Wozniak, and a handful of others, most people, including the authors of this book, missed the computer boat.

Actually, one of us was inspired enough to spend $5 for an Altair 8800 manual which today might be worth at least $10. We should have jumped on the next plane to Albuquerque and offered our services to Ed Roberts.

You get plenty of advance warning

Timing is critical. Yet the paradox is that you generally have plenty of time to ride the Product Horse. If you can recognize a winner, you can take your time to saddle up.

The transistor was invented at Bell Labs in 1947. Almost immediately, it could be seen that the transistor would replace the bulkier, more expensive, and less reliable vacuum tubes that were the key components in any radio or television set.

The strange thing is that nobody did anything about it, at least not in America. The leading American manufacturers were proud of their Super Heterodyne radio sets, which were the ultimate in craftsmanship and quality. These manufacturers announced that while they were looking at the transistor, it "would not be ready" until "sometime around 1979."

Sony was practically unknown outside Japan at that time and was not even involved in consumer electronics. But Sony's president, Akio Morita, saw the potential of the transistor and quietly bought a license from Bell Laboratories to use the transistor for the small sum of $25,000. Within two years, Sony produced the first portable transistor radio—an inexpensive model that weighed only one-fifth as much as a comparable vacuum-tube radio. With prices that were only one-third that of vacuum-tube radios, Sony captured the entire United States market for cheap radios by the early 1950s.

The microwave oven was introduced right after World War II. Thirty years later, in 1976, fewer than 4 percent of American homes had a microwave oven. Then the market exploded. Today more than half of all households have microwave ovens.

At a time when most companies were trying to make existing products microwavable, Jim Watkins had an inspiration. He would create a company devoted to making only microwavable foods.

The time was 1978, and Watkins was a Pillsbury employee assigned to develop microwavable foods for the vending market. Convinced that a big demand existed for microwavable entrees, he left Pillsbury and founded Golden Valley Microwave Foods Inc.

In 1981 Watkins entered the microwavable popcorn market with Act I, a frozen product with real butter in special packaging that allows more complete popping of kernels. The company hasn't looked back since. Its sales totaled just $3.2 million in 1981. Today Golden Valley is a $138 million operation.

The Apple I, for example, was not introduced until July 1976, a year and a half after the Altair 8800 made the cover of *Popular Electronics*. The phenomenally successful Compaq Computer Corp. was not founded until 1982, a year after IBM introduced the PC.

Still, it's important to ride a Product Horse early in the game. By 1988, when Steve Jobs introduced the NeXT computer, it was probably too late. The NeXT machine was left at the starting gate.

How do you recognize a good Product Horse? Good question. First of all, you probably need a little expertise in the product area you're looking at. That's why you're a lot more likely to find opportunity in your own backyard rather than looking for the new and exotic on someone else's turf.

Mike Markkula was an electrical engineer who had worked for Fairchild and Intel, two of the most successful computer chip manufacturers. In October 1976 he visited the garage which Steve Jobs and Steve Wozniak were using to assemble the Apple I. He liked what he saw and two months later joined the company, putting up $91,000 for a one-third interest. (Today it would cost you $1.5 billion to buy a one-third interest in Apple Computer, Inc.)

What Brian Epstein did for the Fab Four, Mike Markkula did for the two Steves. He helped Jobs write the business plan. He obtained a line of credit for Apple at the Bank of America. Even more important, he convinced Wozniak and Jobs that neither had the experience to run a company and hired Mike Scott as Apple's president. (Scotty had worked for Markkula in product marketing at Fairchild.)

Markkula's marvelous track record at Apple brings up another point. It's much better to be cooperative than competitive. Most traditional career-oriented individuals are intensely competitive, especially in large corporate environments. They believe their future depends on beating the person at the next desk.

They may be right ... in the large corporate environment. (This is one of the reasons we are negative about big companies. We find that most career paths in the *Fortune* 500 are marked with dead ends.) There are only a few paths to the top. And the competition for those few golden trails is intense.

But in the world at large, cooperation is a much more effective strategy than competition. Markkula could have looked at Wozniak's handiwork and said, "I'm older, more experienced. I can beat them at their own game."

Maybe. Maybe Mike Markkula could have built a $5 billion computer company all by himself. Then again, maybe not.

Why take a chance? A Product Horse that becomes a

big winner has room for a lot of riders. Furthermore, the more riders whipping that animal, the bigger the potential win.

You can easily afford to share the wealth. (Except to the IRS and your heirs, there's not much difference in life styles between a $10 million winner and a $100 million winner.)

You find your fortune in others, not yourself. Apple itself illustrates the importance of this principle. The key Product Horse at Apple was the Macintosh. As a matter of fact, if it weren't for the Mac, Apple today would be the size of a crab apple rather than the size of a McIntosh.

Not so well known is how the Mac got its mouse, the key feature of the entire new computing system. Again, it's the story of the inventor and the recognizer coming out on top.

In 1978 Jobs went to Xerox and said, "Look. I will let you invest a million dollars in Apple if you sort of open the kimono at Xerox PARC."

The Palo Alto Research Center was the ultimate high-tech laboratory, not that it did Xerox much good. Over the years, PARC spewed out a host of revolutionary computer ideas. Jobs was dying to get a look.

Xerox made two mistakes. They gave Steve Jobs a tour, and they didn't invest the million dollars.

"I was blown away," Jobs said later. What blew him away was an input device conceptually different from anything then in use. The mouse could lead to a new kind of computer system, one much easier to use.

The Mac with the mouse was an enormous success. It established Apple as the company that makes computers that are easy to use. "Of the 235 million people in America, only a fraction can use a computer," said the announcement ad. "Introducing Macintosh. For the rest of us."

"If you can point," continued the ad, "you can use a Macintosh." Today Apple is 90 percent Macintosh and only 10 percent Apple. The Mac was a successful corporate Product Horse for Apple and a personal Product Horse for Steve Jobs, both courtesy of Xerox.

Jobs was already chairman and principal stockholder of Apple, so the Mac success did nothing for him except polish his image. Don't discount the importance of the latter. When you have money, you still might be willing to work hard for a reputation.

Across the country another computer company developed a magnificent Product Horse called the IBM PC. The jockey chosen to ride it was Don Estridge, president of IBM's entry systems division.

What Mustang did for Iacocca, the PC could have done for Estridge. No one will ever know how high he could have ridden the PC horse. Four years after the PC was launched, Steve Jobs offered Don Estridge the chief executive position at Apple with a starting annual salary and benefits package that topped $1 million. This was the job that Jobs later gave to John Sculley.

Estridge was also offered the presidency of Sun Microcomputers, a fast-rising star in the workstation market.

But Estridge's eyes were on the top job at IBM. "All roads must eventually lead to Armonk," he was fond of saying. Many years later IBM chairman John Akers said he believed Don Estridge had the potential to head up all of IBM or at least to be one of the company's six top executives.

We will never know. On August 2, 1985, Don Estridge was killed in a Dallas plane crash.

The future will look a lot like the past

Many people think just the opposite. They assume we live in a world of rapid change. Only a Product Horse from the twenty-first century will do.

Nothing could be further from the truth. In spite of books like *Future Shock*, we still live in houses made of brick or wood or stone, not plastic. We still wear clothing made of wool or cotton, not paper. We still drive cars that look like automobiles, not space ships.

One of the more popular cars on the road today is a Jeep, designed more than 50 years ago. Even mundane products change slowly, if ever. A pencil, a paper clip, and a coat hanger of the thirties would not look out of place in the nineties.

Even when things do change, they often revert to the past. Texas Instruments tried to get us to switch to digital watches with high-tech designs at low-tech prices ($9.95 and less). In case you haven't noticed, most people have gone back to the old-fashioned analog watches at high-tech prices. Rolex sells a lot of watches with Roman numerals on the face for $2000 and up. Mostly up.

Simple concepts are better than complex ones

Simple concepts often have an ominous why-didn't-I-think-of-that quality.

Take Pictionary, the best-selling board game since Trivial Pursuit swept the country in 1982.

Rob Angel was a young man with a bachelor's degree in business administration and two years of experience waiting tables when he remembered the game of charades on paper he used to play at parties.

The game of charades—and its derivative, charades on paper—has been around for centuries. Literally millions of people have played the game at one time or another, but only Rob Angel decided to make a product out of it by adding formal rules, a board, and a box full of word cards. A Product Horse called Pictionary has made Rob Angel a millionaire.

Pictionary illustrates the principle that success is something you find rather than something that springs out of yourself. That's why it's important to keep your eyes open and your ego shut.

Angel found charades and with a little effort turned it into a winning Product Horse. Others found Pictionary and used it as their own personal horse.

Tom McGuire was West Coast sales manager for Selchow & Righter, the toy company that produces Trivial Pursuit, when he noticed a new game called Pictionary that was having some success in the state of Washington. So he bought a copy and gave it to his three grown daughters and their friends to play.

"They were having one wild and wonderful time, a lot of laughter, and a lot of fun," he remembers. That encouraged him to contact Rob Angel about taking the game national. Angel agreed, so McGuire quit his job at Selchow and signed on as Angel's national sales manager.

Sales boomed. But Angel did not have the capital to handle the press runs needed to meet the demand. He started to entertain offers to license Pictionary.

McGuire convinced Joe Cornacchia to get involved. Cornacchia was the printing broker who had helped Selchow & Righter produce millions of copies of Trivial Pursuit. Cornacchia formed a company called the Games Gang, with McGuire as vice president of sales and manager. Together they successfuly bid for the Pictionary rights.

In 1988 Pictionary became the third-best-selling toy in the nation, right behind Nintendo and Barbie.

Angel, McGuire, Cornacchia: all became wealthy because of their ability to recognize a Product Horse. In McGuire's and Cornacchia's case, it was a horse they did not even create.

The pattern of finding a simple product idea and then changing its name to suggest a new and exciting product has been repeated over and over again.

Carl Sontheimer was a retired electronics engineer and dedicated author who haunted the Paris housewares show in 1971, looking for a project to occupy his spare time. He found a powerful, compact French machine that could grind, chop, mince, slice, puree, pulverize, mix, and blend with stunning speed. Sontheimer and his wife Shirley tracked down the machine's inventor, Pierre Verdun, who had also invented its precursor, Le Robot-Coupe, a heavy-duty restaurant machine dubbed the "buffalo chopper" by American chefs.

Sontheimer secured distribution rights for the machine in the United States, then shipped one dozen back to Connecticut to tinker around with in his garage. He refined the French processor's design, improved its slicing and shredding discs, incorporated safety features, and rechristened it the Cuisinart food processor.

Today there are some 30 different brands on the market, but Cuisinart is still the leader.

Another rider who found his Product Horse overseas is John Durso. But he didn't actually leave the country.

Durso's horse is a product called ConForm, polystyrene building blocks used to make poured-in-place concrete walls. Mr. Durso came up with the idea after a chance meeting with an English architect who had seen similar products in Europe. The architect, David Horobin, is now Durso's vice president of marketing. Both men are now riding the ConForm horse.

Less than 5 percent of the world's population lives in the United States. If you're looking for a Product Horse to ride, you might as well cast your eye at the other 95 percent of the world.

The ballpoint pen was invented by the Biro brothers in Hungary, but it was Milton Reynolds who made a fortune by introducing the product in the United States. Reynolds was an entrepreneur who saw the product on sale in Argentina and found a way to circumvent the Biro patent.

Food, clothing, household products—there are thousands of Product Horses waiting to be discovered. And you don't have to spend thousands of dollars on airfares. You can subscribe to a few magazines and let the products fly over to you.

Learn how to say, "That's it."

It's rare for someone to look at an outsider's product and say, "That's it." Normally they say, "Well, that's a pretty good try. Let me make some suggestions. Maybe I can help you whip your idea into shape."

What they are really saying is, "Let me see if I can get myself involved in that product before I agree to jump on and ride it."

That's a mistake. When you find a good Product Horse, forget about trying to get yourself involved and forcing the other person away. Why not just jump on it? Why not say, "That's it. Let's go for a ride"?

You might surprise yourself. You might find that's exactly it. You might find that's exactly the horse that will take you to the top. Don't always try to change everything. Ask yourself, "Why am I trying to change everything?"

Fundamentally you're trying to change everything because you're trying to get yourself into the product. Forget yourself. Evaluate it purely on the basis of whether or not it's a good horse.

Finis Conner was financially set for life with the millions he made as a founder of Seagate Technology. After a falling out with his partners in 1984, he went into retirement. The following year John Squires and Terry Johnson approached him about investing in a new company to make a 3.5-inch disk drive. Mr. Conner, not very enthusiastically, flew to Denver to meet them.

On the way from the airport, the two investors passed the disk drive over the back seat to Conner. "My God," he said, "it's perfect." He jumped in with both feet to form a company called Conner Peripherals.

Currently the fastest-growing major manufacturer in America, Conner Peripherals will surpass $1 billion in revenues after only four years of operation. Conner's stock recently had a market value of $56 million.

If you can't find the product, find the problem

"A problem well stated," said Charles Kettering, "is a problem half solved."

As Edwin Land and his three-year-old daughter walked around Santa Fe, New Mexico, she asked her dad why she couldn't see at once the picture he had just taken. Good question.

Within an hour, the idea for an instant camera and film became so clear to Land that he hurried over to see Polaroid's patent attorney, who also happened to be in Santa Fe. Land described the new product in great detail.

Five years later Polaroid introduced the Land camera, which produced a snapshot in 60 seconds and sold for $89.75. It was an instant success.

Peter Goldmark was listening to pianist Vladimir Horowitz playing Brahms when he blew his stack. What annoyed him was the music being interrupted by the snap-crackle-thump of the record changer. Why not put a full performance on a single disk, he thought?

Record makers, of course, had been trying to do this for years, mainly by increasing the number of grooves on a conventional 78 rpm record. Goldmark decided to create a whole new system.

Wheedling funds out of a skeptical William Paley, the CBS president, Goldmark created the long-playing record. (He picked 33⅓ rpm, the rate used for recorded broadcasts.)

The long-playing record was an enormous success for Peter Goldmark, for CBS, and for the rest of the industry. In the first 25 years, CBS alone took in $1 billion from its LPs.

In Goldmark's case, the irritation factor was an important component of finding a solution to the record changer problem.

At AT&T it was the threat of an operator strike 70 years ago that spurred the company to develop dial telephone service.

The greater the irritation factor, the more likely it will result in some profitable product idea. Don't fight it. Let the irritation factor guide you to a way to solve your own problem.

Josephine Cochrane ran a restaurant. Her staff was always breaking her expensive dishes, so she invented the dishwasher.

Arthur Fry sang in a choir in St. Paul, Minnesota. It bugged him when the bits of paper marking his place in the hymnal kept falling out. One Sunday, he recalled an adhesive a 3M colleague had invented. Unlike most adhesives, this one could be readily detached.

Post-it note pads went on to become one of the five best-selling office products in the world. "I don't know if it was a dull sermon or divine inspiration," quips Fry, who has become something of a celebrity on the lecture circuit.

Note that Fry did not invent the adhesive that made Post-it possible. He recognized the potential of the adhesive to solve a problem he personally experienced.

Frank McNamara was entertaining friends at a New

York restaurant when he was embarrassed to discover he'd lost his wallet with all his cash. So he dreamed up the idea of a credit card called Diners Club.

Leo Gerstenzang was annoyed when he saw his wife trying to clean their baby's ears with toothpicks and cotton, so he thought up the Q-Tip.

George de Mestral took a walk in the woods outside Geneva, Switzerland, and came back with cockleburrs stuck to his jacket. Under a microscope, he found the burrs were covered with tiny hooks which became snared in the fabric loops of his jacket.

His curiosity led to Velcro, which also fastens with tiny hooks and loops. A group of international inventors named Velcro one of the century's most important independent inventions.

Few people can aspire to become a de Mestral, Gerstenzang, McNamara, Fry, Cochrane, Goldmark, or Land. It usually takes a rare combination of circumstance, timing, and experience. In other words, you have to be in the right place at the right time.

But it does no good to be in the right place at the right time if you're so self-oriented that you ignore what's going on outside yourself. In truth, most people are too busy with their own goals, work habits, "to do" lists. Most reasonably capable executives don't have the time to put a cockleburr under a microscope or wonder how a baby's ears ought to be cleaned.

Too bad. If the truth were known, the average person misses dozens of exceptionally fine Product Horses during the course of a working lifetime. The average person has to settle for what fate dishes out. The objective of this book is to give fate a helping hand.

What the de Mestrals, Gerstenzangs et al. demonstrate is the principle of looking outside yourself to find your Product Horse. In practice, however, you are most likely to find yourself living the life of Alan Lefkof.

Lefkof was a 27-year-old consultant at McKinsey & Co. in 1981 when he got a peek at Grid Systems Corp.'s 10-pound laptop computer. "The only other portable computers back then were the 25- to 30-pound types," he says.

Lefkof was sufficiently impressed to quit his McKinsey job and sign on as a Grid sales manager, a bold move at the time considering that McKinsey was the bluest of the blue-chip consulting firms and Grid was almost totally unknown. Soon he was head of marketing, then of finance and corporate development. Along the way he helped engineer Grid's sale to Tandy.

Recently Alan Lefkof was named president of Grid, now a $130 million company. How do you get to be president of a $130 million company at the age of 36? The same way you get to be Vice President of the United States at the age of 41.

Find a horse to ride.

You're never too young

Bill Gates was a freshman at Harvard when his buddy Paul Allen ran across the Altair opportunity. What would you have done?

"Great idea, Paul, but wait till I get my degree." Would that have been your response?

Horses won't wait. When they're ready, they're ready. Would you rather have a Ph.D. from Harvard or be chairman of an $800 million software company?

You don't get rich and famous by dropping out of

college, of course, You get rich and famous by finding a horse to ride. Stay in school. Get your degree. It can't hurt you. On balance it will probably help you.

You should even consider sticking around school and getting your master's degree. Even a Ph.D. if you can afford one.

Wherever you are—in college, working for a company, or working for yourself—you should keep your eyes open. When you see the horse that can take you to the top, don't hesitate. Give up what you're doing and jump on its back. You may never get another chance.

If that means giving up Harvard or Howard or Hofstra, so be it. Horses are rare. Colleges are not. Every September 3300 institutions of higher learning open their doors, rain or shine, to some 2.5 million freshmen.

If your horse stumbles or gets lost on the way to the boardroom, you can always go back to a classroom.

Michael Dell was a freshman at the University of Texas in 1983 at a time when the IBM personal computer was hot. Dell made a key observation.

"The way their system worked," said Dell, "a dealer could order 10 and actually receive just 1. Or sometimes he'd order 100 and only receive 10. So sometimes, even if they only wanted 100, they'd order 1000—and, lo and behold, 1000 would be delivered."

"In those cases," he continued, "dealers would sell me the extra computers at or below cost, just to keep their cash flowing." To get started, he took $1000 from his savings to put together his first deal.

Once he had the computers, Dell would then add on options, such as extra memory and disk drives, then resell the upgraded computers to his fellow students at bargain prices. "In April of 1984, the last month I did business in my dorm room, I did $80,000 worth," he said. "The next month I incorporated and moved into an office."

Dell's next move was to build IBM clones from scratch, but he didn't try to sell them through established computer stores. Instead he looked for another channel which no other computer company was using. That channel was direct marketing. With ads in trade magazines and a staff of operators, Dell sells IBM clones by phone.

Last year the five-year-old company sold $385 million worth. Dell's stock in Dell Computer Corp. is currently worth more than $100 million.

Not bad for a 24-year-old dropout from the University of Texas.

Bill Cunningham was a 17-year-old high school senior in Dallas when he scraped up $700 to launch his direct marketing business. Today at age 21, he's running a 50-employee company which does $1.6 million a year.

Cunningham's brainstorm came in the mail. He noticed several postcards from real estate agents offering to appraise his parents' home and put it on the market.

"The cards were too easy to throw out," said Cunningham. "I thought how much more effective it would be to call homeowners on the phone." So the teenage entrepreneur contacted a big real estate firm and offered to call prospective home sellers and set up free appraisals.

The real estate company agreed and Cunningham was in business. He hired a couple of part-time workers and in the first six weeks he landed 2000 new home sales listings for his client. Later on his firm provided the same service for other real estate companies and Merrill Lynch.

Cunningham's company, Dial USA, also does fundraising for nonprofit corporations, market research, and lead generation for sales organizations. He's not a multimillionaire like Dell, but then again, Cunningham is only 21.

You're never too old

Ray Kroc was 51 years old before he saw the San Bernardino hamburger stand that was going to change his life. He was 52 when he formed McDonald's System, Inc.

Kroc was a paper cup salesman who had briefly tried selling Florida real estate before setting up a company to sell milkshake mixers. He had never run a restaurant, served a hamburger, or sold a milkshake.

No matter. What he was good at was recognizing a good idea when he saw it. He came to San Bernardino to see why the McDonald brothers were buying so many of his mixers. What he saw convinced him to buy the franchising rights for a concept that would conquer the fast-food world.

You're never too old if you look at life with an open mind. Unfortunately, as you get older, you tend to fill up your mind with an enormous array of facts. Pretty soon, you know everything and therefore are in the unfortunate position of not being able to recognize a new product idea, no matter how brilliant.

Too bad. When the two Steves took their baby Apple computer to their bosses at Atari and Hewlett-Packard with the suggestion that their companies take over their prototype product, they were both turned down. Wozniak tried his Hewlett-Packard supervisor on three separate occasions. The older man pointed out that (1) Woz didn't have a college degree or (2) the formal qualifications for a computer designer.

Today both Atari and Hewlett-Packard are into personal computers, but far behind Apple, now a $5 billion company and No. 96 on the *Fortune* 500 list.

We're not talking about a big investment either. When Atari and Hewlett-Packard said no to Apple, they could have launched a personal computer out of petty cash. Radio Shack, for example, invested just $150,000 in tooling, engineering, and software to get its successful TRS-80 Model 1 to market.

The antidote for old age is a suspension of judgment. Don't be too quick to say no. Don't let your superior experience blind you to new opportunities. (Keep asking yourself, "If I'm so smart, how come I'm not rich?")

Jason Epstein was 61 when his big product was born. It took four decades for his idea to germinate.

Epstein is publisher of *The Reader's Catalog*, a "book of books" which just might revolutionize the book business. There has been an enthusiastic response almost everywhere. The book is a selection of such clubs as the Book-of-the-Month Club and the Quality Paperback Book Club.

The idea goes back to Epstein's student days at Columbia University when he "lived" at the Eighth Street

Bookstore in New York's Greenwich Village. "That store had everything you could possibly want," he says. (The Eighth Street Bookstore is long gone, and so are most stores like it, victims of high rent.)

The Reader's Catalog offers more than 40,000 books in 208 categories. What makes the catalog practical is today's low-cost computer technology. Mr. Epstein expects to update and correct the catalog's pages daily.

What's remarkable about the catalog is that Epstein is not a novice. He's been editorial director of Random House since 1958. It's hard to see the forest when your day is spent chopping down trees.

Age and experience usually work against your ability to recognize a good product idea. You become a victim of know-it-all-itus.

Big companies easily fall victim to the disease. That's why radical new products seldom come from any of the industry giants. Six years after the Altair 8800 and four years after the Apple II, IBM finally got around to introducing the PC. Actually this was blinding speed for the Armonk colossus. They beat out all the regular computer players including DEC, NCR, Wang, and Hewlett-Packard

Don't fall in love with the hype

People looking for a Product Horse often make the mistake of falling in love with the hype. When a new product concept is widely talked about in the general press and on television, it's usually a false alarm.

After World War II, the automobile was going to be obsolete. Every house was going to have a helicopter in the backyard, according to the stories in the general media. Unless your name is Trump or Busch, precious few American families have gotten their helicopters.

Also, if you believed the hype, the carpenter, the plumber, and the bricklayer were going to be mostly out of work. Houses were going to be manufactured the modern way, on a production line. Either we're waiting for the Japanese to do it or the press was wildly optimistic. So it went for electronic newspapers, video-text, and the 1-inch-thick television screen.

The truth is, the revolutionary new product idea usually arrives with a whisper, not a bang. The Altair 8800 made the cover of *Popular Electronics,* a relatively obscure publication, not *Time* or *Newsweek.* Further-more, none of the big general-interest magazines or newspapers paid any attention to the Altair article that inaugurated the era of the personal computer. Further-more, the Altair arrived without benefit of press con-ference or publicity agent.

Contrast Altair with Kevlar, a lightweight miracle fi-ber five times stronger than steel. (Sounds terrific, doesn't it?) Du Pont introduced Kevlar with the biggest of big bangs. In 1987 *The Wall Street Journal* reported that after 25 years, $700 million in capital outlays, and $200 million in losses, Kevlar has found only fringe uses in widely scattered markets. It looks like Kevlar is turning out to be another Corfam, an earlier, over-hyped Du Pont disaster.

No new newspaper was ever launched with more hype than *USA Today.* After eight years of losses, the paper still has not had a profitable year. So far *USA To-day* has lost about $450 million.

You'd think Gannett would have learned its lesson.

On September 12, 1988, they went ahead and put up $40 million to launch a television show based on the newspaper. Once again, the media bubbled with enthusiasm. Four hundred and eighty-two days later, *USA Today: The Television Show* was gone, along with the $40 million.

Why do losers get so much hype and winners get so little? One reason is that the hype is not a reflection of the potential of the new product. It's more a reflection of the reputation of the hyper. It was Du Pont, the inventor of nylon, that introduced Kevlar and Corfam. Anything Du Pont does demands media attention.

General Motors does too. That's why the new Saturn car has gotten so much ink. Will the Saturn be a success? If the rule of hype holds true, we're not too hopeful. (The last new car to get the coverage Saturn is getting was the Edsel.)

And who can forget the estimated billion dollars' worth of media coverage generated by New Coke? Unfortunately, the product failed to generate the level of sales to go along with the hype.

Compare Apple and NeXT. The Apple II was launched in 1977 by two no-name college dropouts. Publicity was therefore hard to come by. Nevertheless, the Apple II and its variations went on to become perhaps the most successful single product ever introduced anywhere in the world.

Cut to October 1988. Now a grown-up 33 years old, Steve Jobs has just introduced his NeXT machine, housed in a ribbed black magnesium cube, connected by cable to a 17-inch screen dramatically cantilevered over a swooping support. Demand for press conference credentials has been so great that Jobs has had to print tickets in advance, even though the auditorium can hold several thousand people. All the seats are filled.

All the papers are filled with the big story. Jobs makes the cover of a number of publications. He even gets television time.

Money pours in. IBM gives him $10 million to use his NeXT Step software. Ross Perot puts up $20 million for 16.7 percent of the company. Canon coughs up $100 million for an equal amount.

Money pours out. One hundred thousand to Paul Rand for the four-letter logotype. Millions for three white and sea-green buildings overlooking San Francisco Bay. A 25-foot-wide stairway seems to come out of nowhere. Each employee has a 10- by 10-foot glass office. Aisles are 25 feet wide. The company cafeteria looks like a posh art deco restaurant with gray, black, and white marble. Tinted-glass doors lead to the bathrooms.

The extravagance continues in an expensive robot-run factory in Fremont, California. Each NeXT circuit board is assembled "untouched by human hands" in just 20 minutes.

Will NeXT succeed? Probably not. Success comes not when you need it but when you find it. Jobs needs a success to prove himself; hence the double entendre of the NeXT name. Where is the opening? Apple was the first company to launch a personal computer in a package. NeXT is not the first company to put workstation power in a PC box. Sun, Apollo, Silicon Graphics, and others are already working that field.

All the hype in the world won't overcome the handicap of starting so far behind the pack. Not that hype is bad. Quite the contrary. When you find your Product

Horse, you want to generate as much publicity as possible.

Be prepared for setbacks, however. A truly original Product Horse is not going to be instantly accepted by the media. You're going to have to work hard to get your inch of press. (As Jobs did when he promoted the Apple II.)

When accidents happen

Opportunity arrives when you least expect it. You have to be alert to things taking place outside of yourself, especially to accidents.

In the winter of 1923, lemonade salesman Frank Epperson accidentally left a glass of lemonade with a spoon in it on his windowsill overnight. The lemonade froze, giving Epperson an inspiration for a product he soon patented: the Popsicle.

In the summer of 1988, 23-year-old Joanne Marlowe was getting ready to sun herself on a Lake Michigan beach when a gust of wind picked up her towel and covered her with sand. She hit the roof. A friend said, "Joanne, instead of getting angry, why don't you figure out a fix?"

Instead of relaxing at the beach, Ms. Marlowe spent the rest of the day thinking of ways to develop and market a beach towel with weights in the corners so that they won't flip in the wind. Eight weeks later she had the product on the market. By March 1990 she had sold $4.5 million worth of towels.

Sony chairman Akio Morita liked to listen to music when he played tennis. Every match meant he had to set up speakers, amplifier, and a turntable next to his outdoor court. There must be a better way, thought Morita. Result: The Walkman, one of the most innovative and profitable products Sony has ever introduced.

When bad accidents happen

Life isn't always a bowl of cherries. Accidents happen, sometimes very bad ones.

No amount of positive thinking will change the reality of a bad accident. Our advice is to accept the negative as Ron Kovic did. Often a negative can be turned into a positive.

When you run away from reality, you also may turn your back on opportunity. Face reality, good or bad. Ask yourself, "What can I do about this terrible thing that has happened to me that will make it a positive force in my life and in the lives of others?"

Charles Kettering had a friend who died trying to start an automobile with a hand crank. That was the accident that led Kettering to develop the electric starter, perhaps his best-known invention.

Roy Jacuzzi had a cousin who suffered from arthritis. So Roy mounted a small portable outboard boat engine over the side of the cousin's tub to stir his bathwater. Later he designed built-in nozzles to send jets of a tingling air-water mixture under pressure into the tub. The Jacuzzi was born.

John Linvill has a daughter who has been blind since the age of three. Dr. Linvill used to watch his wife spend three or four hours a day translating books into Braille for Candy's schooling. To replace this laborious process, Dr. Linvill began to experiment with focusing a miniature camera over a line of type, then converting this information into electronic impulses that drove tiny vibrating pins which reproduced the messages on a blind person's fingertips.

The result was the Optacon, which allows a blind person to read at an information flow rate approaching normal speaking speed (about 50 to 90 words per minute).

As a result of John Linvill's invention, thousands of blind people now read electronically. One of them is Candace Linvill Berg. With the help of her Optacon she went through Stanford and earned her Ph.D. in psychology.

A. L. Williams was in college when his dad died. The pain of losing his father was bad enough, but the next devastation came when he discovered that the insurance premium his father had struggled to pay for 20 years had not bought enough insurance to replace his income.

For the next several years, he tried to support his own family and help take care of his mother and two brothers. Those years were tough ones, but the toughest part for Williams was seeing his mother suffer.

At a family reunion many years later, something happened that stunned Williams. His cousin, an accountant, told him about term insurance. He explained that whole life insurance combined death protection with a "forced" savings plan that paid a low rate of interest. This bundled product was much more expensive than the cost of pure death protection. His cousin showed him how he could buy $100,000 of low-cost term insurance for the same premium he was paying for $15,000 of whole life.

In 1977 he formed his own company, A. L. Williams. In only a few short years, A. L. Williams has passed industry giants like Prudential and New York Life to become the No. 1 seller of individual life insurance in America.

Robert Kowalski "cried like a baby" in 1984 when he learned that he faced a quadruple coronary bypass operation. (Just six years earlier, he had undergone a triple bypass.)

His fears were unfounded. He came through the operation with flying colors. Energized by his new lease on life, he declared personal war on cholesterol. The result was *The 8-Week Cholesterol Cure,* a book that has revolutionized the once-staid oat bran business. Published in 1987, Kowalski's book recommends a low-fat diet and regular consumption of oat bran.

What Kowalski invented was the oat bran mania that took over America. The book was the No. 1 nonfiction book of 1988 on *The New York Times* best-seller list. Harper & Row sold more than a million hardcover copies.

When Rabbi Harold Kushner's 14-year-old son died after a long illness, the rabbi asked himself that age-old question, "Why me, God?"

Rather than suffer in silence, he answered his own question with a book published in 1981 entitled *When Bad Things Happen to Good People.* The book sold more than 2 million copies and stayed on the best-seller list for more than two years.

He has since written two more books, which have also become big sellers. "My success continues to astonish me," says Rabbi Kushner, who has served the same Conservative synagogue in Boston since 1966.

Rose Kushner (no relation) gained national recognition in 1975 when she wrote about her battle with breast cancer in the book *Why Me? What Every Woman Should Know About Breast Cancer to Save Her Life.*

She became an influential voice questioning standard medical procedures. Many of the steps she advocated, especially less radical surgery, were at first rejected by leading breast cancer experts but are now common practice.

Tom Houston was a pipe fitter who was paralyzed from the waist down after falling from a scaffold in 1979. With the help of Ray Metzger, also a pipe fitter, Houston used his skills to develop a wheelchair that allows him to stand up. He even uses it to play volleyball with his kids and grandchildren.

His company, Mobility Plus, now markets the $11,500 HiRider. The "walking wheelchair" has done more than just enhance Houston's self-esteem. It is now his livelihood as well.

Robert Kearns got the idea for a "blinking" windshield wiper after losing his sight in one eye. "You begin focusing on your eyes when you've been blinded," he said. "Your eyelids blink. I developed controls that make windshield wipers blink."

Recently Mr. Kearns won a patent-infringement suit against Ford Motor Company. (He has suits pending against most of the world's other car makers, including General Motors.) Theoretically, the loss of an eye could gain him hundreds of millions of dollars.

The Idea Horse

How do you recognize a good idea?

If you're like most people, you compare a new idea to what's already in your mind and then you decide.

"That will never work" is the most common reaction to a new idea. Yet if someone suggests an idea that you have already mulled over in your mind, you're quick to say, "That's a good idea."

You fall in love with your own ideas and are quick to reject the ideas of others. (How do you sell an idea to another person? You try to convince the other person that they thought of it first.)

If you are like most people, you have lots of good ideas. Let us put it another way: You think you have lots of good ideas.

How many of these good ideas have you capitalized on? Was any one of them good enough for you to make a living on? (Probably not, or why would you be reading this book?)

You might not be good at generating ideas, but

surely you are good at judging an idea when it's presented to you.

Everybody is an expert

Judging ideas is an extremely popular pastime. Newspaper space is filled with columns by movie critics, theater critics, art critics, political critics, not to mention daily editorials on a vast array of subjects.

People who heap negative criticism upon all ideas they encounter are often considered to be extremely practical. As a matter of fact, bad-mouthing somebody else's concepts is a cheap way to demonstrate your own mental superiority.

Most companies are organized against ideas. Middle managers see their responsibility to be guarding against possible mistakes rather than nurturing new but fragile ideas.

We were once in a meeting at IBM where a new and fragile idea was being presented. After listening to the presentation of the concept, the executive in charge of the meeting didn't simply make a judgment on whether the idea was good or bad. He looked around the room and announced that the idea was interesting but now the group had to attack the idea and evaluate its weaknesses.

Needless to say, the idea was quickly stomped to death by the other middle-level managers in attendance. Most of the people in the room felt that the safe move was to go with the instructions to attack.

If you want to ride the Idea Horse, you have to resist your critical instincts. The world doesn't really care whether you think the latest Sylvester Stallone motion picture is any good or not. You have to suspend judgment.

It's not easy to do. Your first instinct is to express your opinion. And once you've done that, it's hard to change your opinion because you have to do it publicly.

One of the best ways to suspend judgment is to say something in a noncommital way. "Hmmm, that's interesting" was the favorite remark of one advertising agency chief executive.

Even harder than suspending judgment is changing your mind. The mark of a mental zombie is the fixed opinion which never changes. "If in the last four years," wrote the late Gelett Burgess, "you have not discarded a major opinion or acquired a new one, check your pulse. You may be dead."

Recognizing a good idea

All right, you've suspended judgment and are mentally prepared to change your mind. How do you recognize a good idea that needs nurturing? A fair question that isn't easily answered. But here are some guidelines.

1. Is It a First?

The first one into the mind with an idea has an enormous advantage. Any good idea has a uniqueness about it. If you can look at an idea and say, "No one is doing that," you're off to a good start.

Walter Wriston was head of the overseas division of Citibank when he came up with his first, the negotiable certificate of deposit or CD. This device arose from a transaction with Onassis's father-in-law, Stavros G. Livanos, a friend of Wriston's. Livanos proposed to use his large deposit as collateral for a transaction. Wriston came up with the idea of a certificate that would show a deposit for a fixed time at a fixed rate, and would be fully negotiable simply by endorsement in the same manner as a debenture or bond.

That innovation suddenly made CDs the source of what is today essentially all the financing conducted in the Eurodollar market. It ultimately led to the personal CD.

And, of course, Wriston ultimately wound up with the top job at Citibank, partly as a reward for his innovation.

2. Is It Bold?

Most powerful ideas have an element of risk about them. They tend to make some people in the room very uncomfortable. If no one gets nervous or agitated when the idea is presented, chances are it's not an exciting idea.

When John Reed was appointed to head up Citibank's consumer division, he was appalled to discover that it was losing money. So he cast about for a bold idea to rejuvenate the bank. His choice: automatic teller machines (ATMs) which promised 24-hour banking convenience to the customer and lower costs for the bank.

ATMs were not new. (No idea is really totally new.) But they were new to New York. At the time, ATMs were viewed by most bankers as exotic experiments, best used in suburban areas or in states like Arizona with low population densities.

Reed was the first to bring ATMs to the Big Apple. He bet big on their success. Over five years Citicorp, the parent company, spent $500 million on research and development, most of which went into automatic teller machines for Reed's operation.

Initially regarded with suspicion as heralding a Brave New World where customers lost all human contact, the ATMs went on to become an enormous success, right up there with same-day dry cleaning service.

Reed's reward? What the CD did for Wriston, the ATM did for Reed. A decade later Reed became chairman and chief executive of Citicorp, the largest U.S. commercial bank.

Interestingly enough, one good idea like the ATM can make up for a number of bad ones. Along the way Reed committed several massive blunders. One time Reed blanketed the country with 26 million letters inviting the recipients to become Visa card holders. "They sent applications to everyone, people who were in jail, people who were in bankruptcy, people with atrocious credit histories," says a former Citicorp executive. "Of course, all those people started using [the cards], and of course most of them skipped their payments." The Visa fiasco cost Citicorp $75 million.

Another time Reed decided to acquire a number of mortgage companies, expecting that interest rates would fall and that their long-term low-interest mortgages would be profitable. When interest rates remained high, the bank lost another $100 million.

"John, how dumb can you be?" Reed admitted in an

interview with the press. Never be afraid to make a mistake. All that counts in the long run is that you associate yourself with one big powerful idea.

3. Is It Obvious?

Most powerful ideas, once presented, seem obvious. Someone will probably say, "That's something we've been doing or talking about. That's not new." Don't be put off by that kind of talk. If it's obvious to the group, it will also be obvious to the marketplace, which means it will work that much faster.

In a Beverly Hills brainstorming session in November 1983, Michael Milken came up with the idea of using high-yield securities to buy companies. The junk bond was born.

Using junk bonds, raiders with little money of their own could acquire big companies. Usually it involved setting up a "paper" company of paltry assets to sell junk bonds for the purchase of viable concerns. The assets of the target company were pledged to repay the junk bonds.

Milken soon became one of the best-known figures on Wall Street. The enormous sums of money he raised bankrolled many small companies frozen out of traditional sources, as well as corporate raiders like T. Boone Pickens and Ronald Perelman.

Milken also became rich. In 1987 alone, he made $550 million from his investment firm Drexel Burnham Lambert.

Unfortunately for Milken, his under-the-table dealings with Ivan Boesky did him in. He pleaded guilty to six felony counts and paid a $600 million fine.

Why would a superrich financier like Milken, who personally collected more than $1.1 billion between 1983 and 1987 from Drexel while earning income from other investments as well, fool around playing penny ante games with the likes of Ivan Boesky?

Maybe it has to do with the "extra edge" that some people seek because they don't feel they are quite as capable as the next person. So they cut a few corners by cheating on exams or by doing a little extra shoplifting.

Success is not a search for that extra edge. Success has little to do with personal ability and much more to do with finding a horse to ride. Milken found his with the junk bond, an obvious idea that had been around the fringes of the financial community for decades.

4. Is It Simple?

People admire complexity. They don't trust something that looks too simple. But only simple ideas will work. The most powerful ideas have an elegant simplicity about them. Less is more.

Phil Knight was a runner (his specialty was the mile) at the University of Oregon. It was there he became acquainted with Bill Bowerman, Oregon's track coach, who had very definite ideas about the design of running shoes. Bowerman claimed that American-made shoes were too heavy and clumsy. No serious runner would think of wearing them.

Knight went on to Stanford, where he earned his graduate business degree. But he stayed in touch with Bowerman, keeping him informed of his idea that it might be possible to find a big market in the United States for well-designed running shoes made in Japan. Two years after Knight's graduation, the two men went into partnership. They each invested $500 for 300 pairs of Tiger running shoes made by Onitsuka of Japan and stored them in the basement of Knight's father's house. They started by selling them only in western states, but met such good response that they soon went international.

When the Olympic trials were held in Eugene, Oregon, in 1972, Knight and Bowerman capitalized on being in the right state at the right time. They produced a pair of shoes they had designed themselves and persuaded marathoners to wear them so that they could advertise that Nikes were on the feet of "four of the top seven finishers." (The ads did not mention that the first three finishers were wearing Adidas shoes.)

Today Nike is a $2 billion company and accounts for 26 percent of the domestic athletic shoe market. Nike is a simple idea: American-designed running shoes made in the Far East and sold with a Greek name. (Nike is the Greek goddess of victory.)

5. Will It Upset the Apple Cart?

Good ideas often have a strong competitive angle to them. They tend to put somebody on the defensive. If you can look at an idea and say, "So-and-so will hate that," you could be onto something big.

Anita Roddick is shaking up the cosmetic business. In England in 1976, Ms. Roddick started the Body

Shop where she sold soaps, lotions, shampoos, and creams based on ancient formulas. Pineapple as a skin cleanser, cocoa butter as a moisturizer, Japanese azuki beans ground into washing grains. The products were packaged in simple, refillable plastic bottles with hand-written labels. (It was enough to make Charles Revson turn over in his grave.)

Her company grew rapidly. Today there are 450 Body Shops around the world. At 47, Anita Roddick is already the fourth richest woman in Great Britain. Revlon and Estée Lauder have not gone out of business yet, nor are they likely to. But ...

What Anita Roddick did in cosmetics, Ted Forstmann is doing in finance. His firm, Forstmann Little & Co., was one of the first leveraged buyout specialists on Wall Street ... but with a difference. Unlike Kohlberg Kravis Roberts, Forstmann took a strong position against the use of junk bonds.

In a dozen years, Forstmann Little completed 14 buyouts worth more than $7 billion. In the process, the firm earned tens of millions of dollars. With the folding of Drexel Burnham Lambert and the junk bond market in disarray, Mr. Forstmann's star is definitely rising.

There's room in the marketplace for a variety of approaches, even for those that upset the established apple cart.

"The fact that an opinion has been widely held is no evidence whatever that it is not entirely absurd," wrote Bertrand Russell. "Indeed in view of the silliness of the majority of mankind, a widespread belief is more likely to be foolish than sensible."

6. Is the Idea Timely?

Most people have the wrong idea about ideas. They assume that an idea is a unique experience that occurs to one person, as if we would still be using candles if it weren't for the genius of Thomas Edison.

Not true. "An invasion of armies can be resisted," said Victor Hugo, "but not an idea whose time has come." The trick is to be the first to recognize the fact that the time is ripe for an idea to spread its wings.

While most people live in the past and are woefully behind the times, you can also be ahead of the times. That's bad. In the nineteenth century Charles Babbage devoted most of his life and expended much of his private fortune and a government subsidy in an attempt to perfect a mechanical calculating machine. In essence, Charles Babbage "invented" the computer, but it didn't do him any good. He was ahead of his time.

On the other hand, the newspaper *USA Today* is an idea whose time has come and gone. Right after World War II a national general-interest newspaper might have been a big success. The wars in Europe and Asia had made Americans superaware of the international scene and our role in the world. Newspaper circulation was booming.

By September 15, 1982, when *USA Today* was launched, newspaper readership was declining. The news torch had been passed to television.

Allen Neuharth launched *USA Today* when he was CEO of Gannett Company. His timing was much better with another newspaper.

When Neuharth worked for the *Miami Herald*, he watched the first space rockets take off from Cocoa Beach. He decided that the area would take off too. So he tried to get his employers to launch a new daily newspaper in the Cocoa Beach area. They refused.

He then joined Gannett with a prior agreement to consider a new Florida daily. The new paper, called *Today*, was a big success and propelled Neuharth to the top of Gannett.

Timing was important in the formation of Kohlberg Kravis Roberts, the fabulously successful Wall Street firm. In the mid-sixties Jerome Kohlberg was working at the investment banking firm Bear Stearns where he developed a gimmick called the "bootstrap deal." At the time many of the folks who had founded companies during the postwar economic boom were growing old. They were looking for ways to get their money out and, at the same time, turn the company over to the next generation of managers.

Enter the leveraged buyout or LBO, a kind of aid to the elderly. Working for Kohlberg at the time were George Roberts and his cousin Henry Kravis. Kohlberg proposed to Bear Stearns management that he, Kravis, and Roberts set up a freestanding LBO group within the investment firm. Bear Stearns said no. (Recognizing a good idea when you're handed one on a silver platter is a rare commodity indeed.)

Kohlberg Kravis Roberts went on to become, person for person, the most profitable Wall Street firm ever. In 1988, for example, the average earnings of the top five partners at KKR was $59 million *each*. The following year the company did the RJR Nabisco buyout, which generated fees of $1.1 billion for KKR and its banks and advisors.

Another timely idea was the "poison pill," which allows management to ward off the unwanted advances of raiders. In its simplest form, the pill is the right of a target company shareholder to buy stock in the surviving company at half-price if the raider wins. Invented by Martin Lipton in 1983, the poison pill was designed to help Lenox ward off a hostile takeover.

The poison pill has become a big success in Corporate America. Today some 1200 companies have adopted it. Nor has Lipton done badly. His firm (Wachtell, Lipton, Rosen & Katz) charged Kraft Inc. $20 million in fees for three weeks of work done on the company's 1988 takeover by Philip Morris. Lipton himself makes more than $3 million a year.

Inventing a good idea

It's easier to get rich and famous by recognizing a good idea than by inventing one. The odds are better.

There are millions of self-centered people who are potential sources of the one idea you need to be successful. When you try to do it yourself, the sources shrink to one. Yet it can be done.

Even when you invent an idea by yourself, the inspiration usually lies outside yourself. At a fashion show in New York in 1965, Flori Roberts heard several black models discussing the problem of using makeup meant for white complexions. She was surprised to learn that the models mixed various brands and colors until they hit on shades that worked for them.

Two years later the Flori Roberts cosmetics line became the first cosmetics line for black women to break into the prestige department store market. Today Flori Roberts markets 175 items and does $25 million in annual revenues. Flori Roberts, we should note, is white.

There are many success stories in the television medium that illustrate the importance of finding your inspiration on the outside rather than the inside. Vin DiBona, for example, is executive producer of the hottest new show on television, ABC's *America's Funniest Home Videos*. But where did Mr. DiBona get his idea from?

Japan. He saw Tokyo Broadcasting System's *Fun With Ken and Kaito Chan* at an international television festival and brought a tape with the highlights to ABC. When they watched it, the network executives fell off their chairs laughing. *America's Funniest Home Videos* was born.

With the show's popularity soaring, Mr. DiBona receives more than a thousand tapes a day.

Going back a few years, one of television's true geniuses is Norman Lear, whose biggest hit was the 1971 show *All in the Family*.

Not many people are aware of the fact that Lear's blockbuster was modeled on the British comedy *Till Death Us Do Part*, which also brought social satire to sitcoms by taking on taboo subjects such as racism and homosexuality. Lear's real-life model for Archie Bunker was his own father, who often called young Norman "meathead."

What would you do if your dad repeatedly called you a meathead? You'd probably try to bury the thought and spend the rest of your life paying for therapeutic treatment. Sometimes the negative things that happen to you can be powerful motivating forces in your life ... if you don't try to repress them.

Margaret Sanger watched her own mother die an early death after the rigors of bearing 11 children. Later, as a nurse on Manhattan's Lower East Side, she witnessed the deaths of hundreds of young women in the abortion mills then running.

Any wonder that Margaret Sanger became an advocate of birth control, a term she herself coined? She opened the first birth control clinic in the country in the Brownsville section of Brooklyn. (She was promptly arrested and sentenced to 30 days in the workhouse for "creating a public nuisance.")

Birth control was too powerful an idea for religious denominations and local, state, and federal governments to stop. Ms. Sanger founded the American Birth Control League in 1921 and then organized the first World Population Conference in Switzerland six years later. In 1953 her work led to the formulation of the International Planned Parenthood Federation.

Candy Lightner is a mother whose daughter was killed by a drunk driver. Unfortunately, this is a tragedy that has happened to thousands of other parents.

Unlike others, Ms. Lightner decided to do something. She founded Mothers Against Drunk Driving

(MADD), an organization with perhaps the most inspired acronym since the Committee for the Aid and Rehabilitation of Europe (CARE).

MADD has made a difference. "While our politicians were debating the issue," says Lee Iacocca, "Candy Lightner started MADD and dramatically changed our tolerant attitudes toward drunks behind the wheel."

Selling your idea to an outsider

Many people consider themselves to be "an idea a minute" generator. As they go through life, they spin off literally hundreds of ideas. They really believe they could to be rich and famous ... if.

If they could sell one or more of their ideas, preferably to a big company. If they could get a partner who was willing to put up the money. If they could get someone to help them prepare a business plan. In other words, if someone else would do something, you could achieve your goal.

Life doesn't work that way. If you can't sell yourself on an idea, you're unlikely to sell anyone else. By that we mean, if you aren't willing to devote the better part of your life and your resources to an idea, then it is unlikely that someone else will do so, no matter how promising the concept.

You can't ride the Idea Horse part-time.

So the next time you dream up a great merchandising idea you think Procter & Gamble ought to be willing to pay a million dollars for, ask yourself: Am I willing to devote my life to the idea? If not, forget that trip to Cincinnati.

That's another thing. The bigger the company, the less likely it is to consider an idea from the outside. In the first place, a big company typically has thousands of employees, many of whom are trying to sell their own ideas to the same people you might approach.

Then there's the problem of "What is the idea going to do for me?" You might have a terrific idea that will save or make millions for General Electric, but what is the idea going to do for the person at GE that you're trying to sell? If successful, you get the credit. If unsuccessful, the GE person who endorsed your idea gets the blame.

Forget about trying to sell your idea to someone else. Try to sell it to yourself.

Protecting and nurturing an idea

Once you've found an idea to ride, your next assignment is to protect and nurture it. Ideas are most vulnerable in the early phases. Someone can always find something wrong with an idea.

The problem is particularly difficult in a big company environment. You're going to have to work exceptionally hard to ride the Idea Horse on a *Fortune* 500 track. First you have to keep the nay-sayers at bay.

Ideas are rarely born perfect. The wrinkles have to be worked out. Ideas often start out as ugly ducklings before they grow into beautiful swans. Also, ideas rarely cover 100 percent of a problem. Especially if it's a big complex problem. You're better off with a good idea that deals with half a problem than a half-baked idea that deals with the entire problem. Besides, ideas that promise to be all things to all people tend to end up as mush.

So, as valid objections are raised, look for ways to adapt the idea to deal with the problems rather than sit back and let the idea get stamped out. Be careful, however, not to let too many compromises destroy the essence of the concept. If this happens, you'll end up with a stillborn idea that does no one any good.

Once you've nurtured the idea to a point where it begins to stand on its own, your next move is to establish ownership. At a race track you take some of your money and buy a ticket. In a company you wager some of your reputation. You've got to be willing to stand up and say that you think this idea will work. And insist that until someone has a better one, it should be pursued.

In other words, you make a personal commitment to the idea. Whether this is done with memos or presentations or closed-door meetings, it's important that corporate management knows that you are the sponsor of this idea. What you don't want to do is to drop the idea on your superior's desk and let him or her decide whether to run with it or not. That way you're giving up your ownership.

What you should do is to involve your boss and make sure that you carry the idea upward with your superior's blessing. Most bosses are timid when it comes to bold moves. They usually are only too happy to send you in to the big boss to defend the idea. Besides, you have a rationale for staying attached. After all, as the sponsor, who understands your idea better than you do?

Running the corporate gauntlet

Once you've convinced the big boss that your idea has merit, you have to get ready to run the corporate gauntlet. You see, very few big bosses just say, "Great, let's do it." Most will send you out to show your idea around and get some feedback from the other players and departments. It's the old consensus-building game that enables the big boss to have some protection in case things go wrong. It's called spreading the responsibilities, or protecting your corporate assets.

What you've got to realize in advance is that a lot of your fellow corporate players are going to raise their eyebrows when you arrive. To them, you've just become a serious competitor on the corporate ladder. They won't necessarily see your idea as being good for the company. They'll see it as being good for you and your career. This will upset the established pecking order. If your idea clashes with their personal agendas, you've got a problem. In short order, you'll begin to hear about difficulties with your idea and how it doesn't quite fit into the corporate plans.

Take none of their objections lightly. Be friendly. Thank them for their help and ask them to submit their objections to you in writing. (That will usually head off the more stupid objections.) If they're bold enough to put their objections in writing, you then respond in writing to each one.

Also, when you do get an agreement from your associates who aren't threatened, make sure they document their agreement. Get each of them to write you a memo. You should then bundle up the memos and report back to the big boss with a well-ordered consensus presentation. Make sure you list the pros and cons and name names. While they like consensus, most big bosses also recognize the players who have personal axes to grind. They've probably seen those axes ground a number of times.

Implementation and funding

If your idea survives the gauntlet, your final task is to see that it is implemented and funded properly. An idea that isn't properly dramatized or advertised won't get much attention in today's overcommunicated society. You've got to build the case for enough resources to get the idea around the first bend with you aboard.

You might have to build into the program some way of measuring results. That way you've got something to wave around when you need some additional money for reinforcements.

After all that work, it would be a shame if your idea never got a good start out of the gate.

The
Other-Person Horse

Very early in life, a kid learns that there are just three ways to make money: (1) marry a rich person; (2) steal in a nice, clean, legal way; or (3) get to know the right people.

Some kids find a way to marry rich and usually regret giving up love for money. Other kids find a way to steal that turns out to be not quite as legal as they had thought. But most of them ignore the third way. They figure they have to do it themselves.

Too bad. You should get to know the right people. Aside from the Family or Spouse Horse, it's the best way to the winner's circle.

As a matter of fact, the Other-Person Horse is the ultimate horse for most people, since it's difficult to combine your love life with a career and almost impossible to select your parents. At the same time, the Other-Person Horse is one of the trickiest rides in the success sweepstakes.

So great care must be taken in selecting and riding a

person to glory and success. The rewards, however, can be mind-boggling.

No one in Robert Swanson's family had ever finished college. He was going to break the pattern. The school he selected (Massachusetts Institute of Technology) was the most prestigious technical college in the country.

Good choice. The brand-name college would turn out to be very helpful when he selected his horse.

As an MIT freshman, Swanson's grades put him in the lower third of his class. Not an auspicious start. As a senior, he switched from chemistry to management. After graduating from MIT's Sloan School of Management, he joined a brand-name bank, Citibank. Another good choice.

Four years later Swanson found his third horse: Kleiner & Perkins, the legendary San Francisco venture capital firm whose start-up successes included Compaq, Lotus, Tandem, and Sun Microsystems.

Swanson didn't last long at Kleiner & Perkins. He did, however, last long enough to get interested in the infant science of gene-splicing.

Two years earlier two biochemists, Herbert Boyer and Stanley Cohen, cut strands of DNA from two separate organisms, stuck them together, and created the world's first clone. Boyer and Cohen dubbed their new technique "recombinant DNA."

Swanson was 28 years old when he zeroed in on his fourth horse, Herbert Boyer. At the end of their first meeting, both had agreed to put up $500 each to form a partnership to exploit recombinant DNA technology. Swanson would handle the money and the marketing.

Boyer, who would later win a Nobel Prize, would manage the scientific research.

Boyer's research produced results. Genentech was responsible for four of the first six biotechnology products to hit the market: human insulin, alpha interferon, human growth hormone, and the clot-dissolving drug TPA.

Less than five years after his first meeting with Herbert Boyer on October 14, 1980, Swanson struck gold. Genentech went public in the most widely anticipated stock offering in history. At the end of the day, Robert Swanson was worth nearly half a billion dollars.

He was 32 years old.

Swanson's success illustrates the importance of being in the right place at the right time. No question about it. If you want to be successful today, your timing has to be right. But it doesn't have to be perfect. Herbert Boyer represented a window of opportunity, the Other-Person Horse, for somebody. As a scientist, he was unlikely to commercialize his ideas on his own.

The window of opportunity stayed open for more than two years. How many people read about gene-splicing and recombinant DNA and decided to do nothing? (At least 10 million people read about the world's first clone in the *National Enquirer* alone.) How many people said, "That's interesting, but I'm not a biochemist"? Swanson wasn't either.

Life moves in slow motion. New opportunities drift into view and then drift out again. But the process can take months or even years.

Everyone is born at the right time and in the right place. The problem is to recognize an opportunity as it drifts into view and before it gets away from you, something that Swanson was very good at.

Forget about yesterday. So what if you weren't working on Wall Street when investment banking was practically a license to steal. So what if you weren't living in Silicon Valley when almost every computer start-up produced a gusher of a millionaire.

Today is today. You won't find today's opportunities in yesterday's successes. (That's the corporate road up Career Mountain, which is rocky and dangerous.) You have to keep an open mind. Who can I ride to the top today, not yesterday?

Tom Perkins did. Even though his venture capital company Kleiner & Perkins parted company with Swanson, he didn't write him off. When Swanson approached him, Perkins put up $100,000 to help launch Genentech.

Perkins' bet paid off. The day the company went public Perkins' four-year-old investment was worth $350 million. The story doesn't end there. In addition to his millions, Thomas J. Perkins also became Genentech's chairman.

Perkins rode Swanson. Swanson rode Boyer. One of your absolute best bets is the Other-Person Horse. Where do you find one of these powerful animals?

Finding a boss to ride

Your boss is the logical place to start. We'll go further than that. If you're not working for the right person, you should immediately send out SOS signals and get ready to abandon ship. The relationship between you and your boss represents the biggest single factor (positive or negative) in your entire career. Select bosses carefully. (Perkins was Swanson's boss.)

You should give more thought to the person you work for than the company you work for. Is he or she going anywhere? If not, who is? Always try to work for the brightest, most competent person you can find. If your boss is going places, chances are good that you are too.

Believe it or not, some people like to work for incompetents. We suppose they feel they will stand out better if their boss is a jerk. Usually it's the opposite. Top management tends to see the entire team as under par. If they become dissatisfied with an operation, they often throw everybody out.

How do you select a boss to ride? What attributes should you look for?

If you were to ask a professional "people person" such as a head hunter what attributes make a person successful, you probably would get answers like integrity, intelligence, skill, and self-confidence. These are all important things to possess, but to us they are just basics. A lot of people possess the basics, yet aren't good bosses to ride. Here are some of the things you should look for beyond the basics.

1. A Little Laziness

Workaholic, check-every-detail bosses are not good candidates. Deep down they would rather do everything themselves. You can never forge an indispensable bond with this type of boss. Find one that's a little bit lazy.

This type of person will let you do a lot more than

the "do everything" type. Over time, you will be able to impress your leader with your abilities, and he or she will rely on you more. If you are to stay aboard for the long ride, you need to establish this kind of reliance.

2. A Little Deviousness

Your person to ride shouldn't be an Eagle Scout. The real world doesn't consist of bright-eyed people looking for old ladies to help across the street. While there are a few of those, they are in the minority. Most of the people out there are shifty-eyed people looking for ways to help themselves at the expense of others. Being a little tricky or roundabout is often a better way to operate in the presence of these types. When your prospective boss's adversaries are never quite sure what he or she is up to, your candidate has an advantage. So if your boss is a little on the slippery side, you're in good hands.

3. A Lot of Political Acumen

Corporations aren't rational organizations. They are collections of egos. Being able to work around these egos is a critical skill that few bosses have. It requires an ability to read people accurately. It also calls for a willingness to submerge one's own ego when it could get in the way. Your candidate should exhibit this ability, especially if he or she works for a big company. There is more politics going on at General Motors than in the U.S. Senate, the House of Representatives, the State Department, and the White House combined.

4. A Warrior Mentality

Find a boss who knows how to win the important battle. It's a competitive world out there, and it's getting worse every year as business spans the globe. (We wrote a book on this phenomenon called *Marketing Warfare*.) If your candidate is a courageous type who's quick to pick up a sword and gallop into the fray, you might have a winner. But before you make your bet, hang back and see if he or she wins a few. Dead warriors make bad horses.

5. Plenty of Out-Front Skills

The ability to lead a charge can make all the difference in winning or losing. Your boss horse should demonstrate an ability to generate enthusiasm. Some call this a "cheer leader" type, but we call it a good salesperson. Ronald Reagan was the consummate "out-front" type. He could communicate and sell his ideas. Who cares about his long naps or lack of attention to detail? (Remember, a little laziness is a virtue in a boss.) He was a horse to ride.

You'll notice that we never listed niceness, generosity, or warmth as attributes to look for in a boss. Unfortunately, those are lovely virtues for human beings to have, and while they might be necessary for salvation, they aren't necessary for success. As generals, Napoleon and Patton weren't very lovable, but they certainly were horses to ride. You'll probably never meet more difficult CEOs than Charles Revson and Jack Welch, but they were business horses to ride. Working for Donald

Trump and his ego can't be all sweetness and light, but he has taken his team for quite a ride (up *and* down). The old line about nice guys finishing last has a ring of truth to it.

How should you treat a boss? Flattery is the key tactic. Climbing the corporate ladder is much easier if you ingratiate yourself with your boss.

Ronald Deluga, a psychology professor at Bryant College in Rhode Island, surveyed 124 enlisted men and women in the Army and found a high correlation between those who engage in ingratiating behavior and those who have acquired favored in-group status with the powers that be. (The Army, Deluga argues, serves as a good proxy for a corporate hierarchy, a conclusion with which we both heartily agree.)

How do you butter up a boss? Flattery, of course, but it's best not to be too direct. Deluga suggests you identify an individual who interacts often with the target and tell that person good things about your boss. (It could be a coworker, your boss's superior, or your boss's secretary.) He or she will pass it on.

Should you ever disagree with a boss? Sure, says Deluga, but only if you yield gracefully later. Bosses feel good if they can persuade you to change your mind.

Flattery pays. Big bosses who are big spenders can be very generous to their key lieutenants. Ronald Perelman, chairman of Revlon, pays each of his three key aides, Donald Drapkin, Howard Gittis, and Bruce Slovin (all lawyers), more than $10 million a year.

When Steve Ross merged his company, Warner Communications Inc., with Time Inc., he rewarded his key people with huge sums. Robert Morgado, executive vice president, got about $16 million. Deane Johnson, office of the president, and Marty Payson, general counsel, got about $20 million each. Bert Wasserman, chief financial officer, got about $21 million.

Shooting for the top

An even better horse to ride is your boss's boss's boss. In other words, start at the top. This is a tricky one to execute. You have to be subtle and bold, both at the same time.

In a giant corporation, it's almost axiomatic that the next CEO will be someone who was discovered by the current CEO *very early* in his or her career and then was groomed for the job. (You can't just jump on the fast track. Someone has to put you there.) Ability may well be a marginal consideration.

How do you get noticed by a CEO five or six layers above you? Or even more difficult, how do you get noticed by the CEO of a company you don't work for?

Norio Ohga was a budding opera singer at Tokyo University of Arts in the fifties when he was asked to try out some tape recorders sent over by Sony's Akio Morita. Alone among the students, Ohga insisted the recorders could be better. (What better way to get Morita's attention?)

Morita saw to it that Sony helped pay for the nervy baritone's training. A few years later, in 1959, Ohga joined Sony as the head of the tape recorder division. Later he ran CBS-Sony.

When Morita's brother-in-law, Kazuo Iwama, Sony's

president, died in 1982, Ohga succeeded him. It took 23 years for Norio Ohga to reach Sony's second-highest rung. It's safe to say that Akio Morita was watching him every step of the way.

If you work for General Motors, does Robert Stempel know your name? If you work for Citicorp, does John Reed know your name?

"Well, I'm young," you might be saying to yourself, "I've just been here a few years." That's no excuse. You have to find a way to get noticed at the top. Norio Ohga was in his twenties when he met Akio Morita.

Tom Vanderslice was an obscure section manager at General Electric when he was assigned two minutes for a presentation in the chairman's office. His two minutes were so provocative that Chairman Fred Borch invited the young manager to join him for lunch. The meteoric rise of Vanderslice had begun. He became one of six senior GE vice presidents, just losing out to Jack Welch for the top job.

Andy Warhol was wrong. The day won't come when everyone will be famous for 15 minutes. But everyone is likely to receive a few minutes of opportunity to be famous. Winners seem to have the ability to make the most of their 15 minutes.

When you work for a big company, getting noticed is half the battle. That's why you're much better off at headquarters than out in the field somewhere where your only chance to get noticed is by sending in reports. (There's the sad story of a soldier who faithfully wrote his girl every day and came home to find she had married the mailman.)

When you search through the threads of a successful

career, you invariably find a top management connection very early on. John Opel, who ended his IBM career as chairman, was once administrative assistant to Tom Watson, son of IBM's founder. Whatever you do, try to stay as physically close to the center of power as possible. Out of sight, out of mind. Out of mind, out of luck.

It also helps to look the part. Don Kendall joined Pepsi-Cola in 1947 as a fountain syrup salesman. Ten years later he was named president of Pepsi's overseas operations. (In 1965 he became CEO of PepsiCo, Inc.)

Early in his career, Kendall came under the influence of the legendary marketing man, Alfred Steele. The two men worked closely together on a number of projects before Steele gave him the international company to run. Kendall speculates that he might not have gotten the job if Steele had bothered to check his age. Kendall had gray hair at the age of 17 and looked considerably older than his 36 years. Steele later said he thought Kendall was in his mid-forties at the time.

David Ogilvy once remarked that a rising young account supervisor owed part of his good fortune to being totally gray at the age of 30.

Younger women, in particular, might want to re-evaluate the common practice of dyeing their hair to cover the gray. When you're young, you're better off if you look old. When you're old, of course, it's time to look young again.

Finding an associate to ride

In 1985, in a bar after work, Susan Rose, then a 31-year-old art director at J. Walter Thompson and, what's

more important, a chronic doodler, first sketched the
character on a cocktail napkin. Just 15 lines: a triangu-
lar head with features as uncomplicated as a snowman's
and eight locks of scary, stand-up hair.

Her associate, Joanna Ferrone, a 35-year-old owner
of a stock photo agency, named the character Fido,
which they liked because of the suggestion of old-
fashioned dependability. Rose added Dido because she
like the sound, Fido Dido.

Today their Fido Dido character has grown into an international superstar, decorating some $40 million worth
of retail merchandise annually in 16 countries around the
world. Licensed by United Media, which also syndicates
cartoon celebrities like Snoopy and Garfield, Fido Dido
decorates everything from T-shirts to socks, watches, and
hair dryers. There's even talk about a Fido Dido Saturday
morning television program.

What would you do if an associate of yours sketched
an idea on a napkin?

Most people who work together see their associates
as competitors, not collaborators. It's a shame. You usually have much more to gain by looking at the people
around you as potential horses. A lone wolf may make a
lot of noise, but usually never gets very high on the ladder of success.

Like love in a marriage, the cement that holds associates together is mutual respect. Without mutual respect, you'll have a tough time sticking together. The
key question to ask yourself before jumping on the
Other-Person Horse is: "Is this a person whose opinion
I respect?" Forget talent. Forget ability. You'll part
company at the first fork in the road if you don't have

mutual respect. (We explore this concept in more detail in Chapter 10: "The Partner Horse.")

Finding a friend to ride

The hardest horse to recognize is a friend. You know too much about your friends, and the more you know about a person, the less likely you are to recognize a true genius. Up close, people never look quite as capable as they do from afar.

Too bad. Friendship is a good way to get to know a wide range of different kinds of people. Furthermore, it's usually a lot easier to approach a friend than it is a business acquaintance.

Down at the pool, the tennis court, or the golf club, it's easy to say: "I was thinking about starting a computer software company. Are you interested?" Your friend may not be interested but will usually be flattered to be asked.

"But I don't have any friends who are going anywhere," you might be thinking. Are you sure? After the fact, after a person has achieved a measure of greatness, the press often searches out his or her high school or college friends.

"Just an average person" is the typical reply. "I never imagined she (or he) would become so successful."

Surprise! That's the word that describes the reaction of friends and acquaintances. They may lie: "I always knew he (or she) would be a big deal." But deep down, they are always surprised.

Why is it so hard to evaluate a friend? You see the faults but ignore the strengths. Somehow you have to get beyond the surface flaws and concentrate on the other person's strong points. It's worth it to make the effort. You have a natural advantage.

It's easier to jump on board a friend than a stranger. A friend is someone who trusts and respects you. Many associates and managers of celebrities were friends of the celebrities in their youth. Who else can a celebrity trust?

Look around you. It's not always necessary to go to New York or L.A. to find your fortune. The easiest person to overlook is a friend in your own hometown. Furthermore, the longer you have known a person, the longer you have been friends, the less objective you are likely to be.

Paul Allen first met Bill Gates in 1968 in the science lab at the Lakeside School, a Seattle prep school. Seven years later, Allen quit his job and Gates dropped out of college to found Microsoft Corp. Still in their thirties, each is now a billionaire.

They're still friends. They still hang out together, on average, three times a week. In 1988 Allen, a fervent basketball fan, bought the Portland Trail Blazers for about $70 million. Gates is often a guest at the games.

When Allen launched a new software company (Asymetrix Corp.), he recruited a friend and fraternity brother (Bert Kolde) to be executive vice president and manage operations. The earlier the better, but it's never too late to ride the Friendship Horse.

Jon Peters was a hairdresser in his late twenties on Rodeo Drive in Beverly Hills when he met and moved in with Barbra Streisand. She became the friend who would later take Peters to the top.

At the time, agent Sue Mengers had been pushing Streisand to do a remake of *A Star Is Born*. Streisand wasn't interested so Mengers took her case to Jon Peters. "This is a fantastic piece. You could look terrific," he told Streisand. Then Jon Peters set out to produce the movie on his own. Unpopular with the critics, *A Star Is Born* still grossed $140 million — Streisand's biggest box-office success ever. The album alone sold 8 million copies.

A producer is born.

Riding the Celebrity Horse

The hottest pair in television today are Marcy Carsey and Tom Werner. At one point in time, their Carsey-Werner Company had the three biggest hits on television.

What put Marcy Carsey and Tom Werner on top? Bill Cosby did. During its six years on the air, *The Cosby Show* has been almost singlehandedly responsible for NBC's No. 1 position in prime-time network ratings.

How did the duo get Bill Cosby? As unbelievable as it might seem, nobody else wanted him. Half-hour comedy series were considered dead by the three networks. ABC and CBS turned the idea down. NBC eventually agreed to buy the Cosby show, but with reservations.

The Cosby Show has become the biggest jackpot in television history. In just three years, the show has generated almost $600 million in profits from syndication to television stations. As the show's primary owners, Carsey and Werner will retain at least a third of the profits.

One thing leads to another. First there was the Cosby spin-off, *A Different World*, starring Lisa Bonet. Then came another No. 1 show, *Roseanne*, starring Roseanne Barr. Carsey-Werner's success illustrates an important principle for anyone looking for a way up the ladder.

You just need one. By that we mean you just need one major achievement and the rest is easy. Carsey-Werner had to go out and sell themselves to both Bill Cosby and one of the three television networks, not an easy task. But after the success of *Cosby,* everybody came to them. The networks, the stars, the writers, the directors, everybody was lined up to get on board the Carsey-Werner bandwagon.

That illustrates another principle. Failures don't count. In the B.C. years (Before Cosby) Carsey-Werner managed to get only one pilot on the air, *Oh Madeline,* starring Madeline Kahn. It ran on ABC for one season but was not renewed. Who remembers *Oh Madeline?* Who cares?

While Carsey-Werner made a bundle on the Cosby Horse, it isn't necessary to strike it rich on your first outing. All that's necessary for future success is to get a good ride out of your first horse.

William Novak was paid a paltry $80,000 for writing *Iacocca,* a book that sold an astonishing 2.7 million copies. (In the process, the book made $10 million to $15 million for its subject.) Since *Iacocca,* however, Novak has done much better.

For *My Turn,* a book he wrote with Nancy Reagan, he received a six-figure advance plus a hefty percentage of the royalties. As expected, *My Turn* went to the top of the charts and, so far, has sold more than half a million hard-cover copies. Novak has also written *Mayflower Madam* with Sydney Biddle Barrows and *Man of the House* with Tip O'Neill.

Who is William Novak? Before *Iacocca* he had spent ten years editing scholarly magazines and writing a string of financially unsuccessful books. After *Iacocca,* he became, according to *Time* magazine, "the golden mouthpiece of the nation's celebrities."

Failures don't count. All you really need for a long, successful career is one winning horse. Then you just keep doing more of the same.

Ego does count. It counts against you. One of the reasons for Novak's success with celebrities is his self-effacing quality. According to *Time* magazine, "He is a most unassuming, amiable sort who leaves his ego at the door." (Who else would have been able to deal with Lee Iacocca?)

Ego, of course, is something you're born with. Maybe you can raise it a notch or two by reading books like *The Power of Positive Thinking*. But this is all surface work. Underneath, most people remain true to themselves, whether they are ego-driven maniacs or the self-effacing type. To ride the Celebrity Horse, you have to put the brakes on your own ego, at least on the surface. You have to deflate the exaggerated notions of your self-worth.

10

The Partner Horse

Many ideas grow better when they're transplanted into another mind rather than the one in which they sprang up. It's no accident this book was written by two people. Only in a give-and-take atmosphere can ideas be refined and perfected.

It's like basketball. One partner takes a shot and the other partner plays the part of the backboard. If it's a good idea, swish. If the idea is off target, the other partner bounces it back with a different slant.

In certain professions, partnership is an established tradition. Music, television, motion pictures, for example. What we foresee, however, is an era in which the partnership concept is much more universal. Business partners, government partners, all sorts of partners might become much more common. Who knows, someday we might even elect a President and a Vice President who have been partners most of their political lives, instead of electing two people who first met on the floor of the convention.

Why not? Partnership is a powerful principle. If finding a horse to ride is the key to success, then the right combination of partners is going to double or quadruple the chances.

Let's look first at three professions where partnerships are firmly entrenched.

Music partners

Traditionally, the music business has been populated by partners. Typically, one person would write the words; the other, the music. But a good music partnership is more than a division of responsibilities. Good partners work together to create their musical magic.

Richard Rodgers outlived two monumental partnerships. He studied at Columbia, where he met both of his partners. His first was Lorenz Hart.

Rodgers and Hart began to produce smash Broadway musicals in the twenties and thirties: *The Girl Friend, A Connecticut Yankee,* and *Pal Joey.* Their collaboration continued through seven Hollywood films until Hart's death in 1943.

Richard Rodgers' next partner was Oscar Hammerstein II. Rodgers and Hammerstein's first effort was the Pulitzer Prize-winning hit, *Oklahoma!* They continued to write and produce a string of record-breaking musicals, including *South Pacific, The King and I,* and *The Sound of Music.*

Many other creative twosomes have dominated the music industry, such as George and Ira Gershwin and Alan Jay Lerner and Frederick Loewe, whose *My Fair Lady* ran for more than six years on Broadway.

A partnership is a business marriage, and when a marriage breaks up, the results can be devastating.

Paul Simon and Art Garfunkel were born within three weeks of each other in Forest Hills, Queens. By the time they were 14, they were singing doo-wop with a local group. At 23, they cut their first album. At 24, they had their first No. 1 hit, *The Sounds of Silence*. They were on their way to becoming the most commercially successful folk-pop act of the day.

Hit followed hit. *Homeward Bound* and *I Am a Rock*. The theme song *Mrs. Robinson* from the film *The Graduate*. Then they did the album *Bridge Over Troubled Water*, which won five Grammy Awards and sold 15 million copies. It would be their last record together.

At the age of 29, Paul Simon and Art Garfunkel went their separate ways. Their recording career together had lasted only six years, but it was long enough to ensure their induction into the Rock and Roll Hall of Fame. In the 20 years since the break-up, neither has come close to the success they had when they were together.

Simon wrote the songs, yet Garfunkel sang most of the solos. It's a common problem in a partnership. One of the partners is the creative one; the other partner gets most of the credit. "I wrote the song," said Simon about *Bridge Over Troubled Water*, "that I knew Garfunkel was going to sing. But it was such a huge hit, I was standing off in the wings, and the full impact of the hit was going to be Artie."

Success killed Simon and Garfunkel. Any wonder that many wonderful, productive partnerships break up? To keep things together requires that one or both partners swallow a little pride from time to time. Ego is the source of your drive to succeed, but unless it is kept in rein, ego can destroy you.

When you find the horse that takes you to the top, don't change horses. "It was all over after *Bridge*," said Simon. "We were so young we didn't realize we were on the trip of a lifetime."

The same principle applies to the split between Bryant Gumbel and Jane Pauley, which cost the NBC *Today* show its morning leadership. If it ain't broke, don't fix it.

Television partners

The power of a partnership is in the interaction between the two people. The whole is greater than the sum of the partners. It's what multimedia people call "the third image," the picture that's created in the middle of dissolving from one slide to another.

Look at Marcy Carsey and Tom Werner. In one season their Carsey-Werner Company produced the three top-ranked TV shows: *The Cosby Show, Roseanne,* and *A Different World.*

Before forming her own production company, Ms. Carsey was the executive in charge of series at ABC. Mr. Werner was her top aide. When she left in 1980, he succeeded her. The following year he took out a second mortgage on his home to raise money to join Ms. Carsey in her fledgling company, which became Carsey-Werner.

Nine years later, both mortgages are presumably paid off. In any event, he is the principal partner in a group that just bought the San Diego Padres for $75 million. He can afford it. His personal wealth has been estimated at more than $120 million. Mr. Werner, by the way, is 39 years old.

No company we know of hires partners with a joint responsibility and a joint salary. (How would they handle the health insurance forms and the annual performance reviews?) Maybe it's a good idea whose time is coming. At the very least, it might prevent the Carsey-Werners of this world from leaving to do their own thing.

The television industry comes the closest. Most of the major producers of TV shows hire teams to develop their series. Tom Miller and Bob Boyett are a team who developed some of the most successful shows, first at Paramount and currently at Lorimar. Together Miller and Boyett created *Laverne and Shirley, Mork and Mindy, The Hogan Family*, and *Perfect Strangers.*

Barbara Corday and Barbara Avedon are another legendary television team. Their relationship produced *Cagney and Lacey*, the long-running, highly acclaimed series about a pair of policewomen who are close friends as well as partners.

Motion picture partners

The current kings of the Hollywood hills are a pair of Peters. Jon Peters and Peter Guber, the moguls who brought you *Rain Man, Batman*, and *The Color Purple*. Sony recently bought their production company (Guber-Peters) and installed them as cochairmen of Columbia Pictures Entertainment.

The price was a princely one. For a business they had started in 1980, Sony paid $200 million, of which $54 million went to Guber and Peters. At Columbia they will each receive a salary of $2.75 million a year, with cost-of-living adjustments as well as profit sharing and a share of a $50 million bonus. In addition, they will split 8.08 percent of any appreciation in Columbia's assessed value.

Mr. Guber is a second horse for Jon Peters, the Hollywood hairdresser who rose to fame by producing a Barbra Streisand movie. With two law degrees and an MBA, Peter Guber has the credentials and the experience (he once was head of production at Columbia) to turn the studio into a winner. Only time will tell. Either way Guber and Peters will win. They got most of their money up front.

Don Simpson and Jerry Bruckheimer are another Hollywood team who have made it big. Simpson and Bruckheimer, producers of *Flashdance, Top Gun,* and *Beverly Hills Cop,* have just signed an unprecedented five-year contract with Paramount Pictures. The studio is writing them a $300 million blank check for the production of five films which the partners can choose, cast, and promote with no oversight by Paramount. "They put up the money, we put up the talent, and we all meet at the theater," said Simpson.

Ismail Merchant and James Ivory have been making movies together for 27 years. Their biggest hit was the 1986 film *A Room With a View,* which won three Academy Awards. Actually, Merchant Ivory Productions has a third partner who has been associated with the company since the beginning. She is Ruth Prawer Jhabvala, who writes screenplays in addition to her responsibilities for costumes and art direction.

Another profitable motion picture partnership is the one between Gene Siskel and Roger Ebert. Their

show *Siskel & Ebert* reaches over 175 markets and is the
most successful movie review program. The two review-
ers have been working together for a dozen years.

Partners don't have to be buddies. Siskel and Ebert
don't hang out socially. (Ebert is single; Siskel is married with children.) They only meet once a week to do
their show. But their relationship has been profitable.
Their salaries are over $1 million a year apiece, plus
what they make on their newspaper jobs. (They work
for rival Chicago newspapers.)

Business partners

Except for entrepreneurs, long-term partnerships are
rare in the corporate world. For one thing, it's hard to
fit two partners into one box on an organization chart.
Why not? Why not work with a permanent partner,
even in a large corporation? This is uncharted water
which might turn out to be very productive for pioneer
partnerships.

Advertising agencies have flirted with the partnership concept for years. They often assemble creative
teams consisting of an art director and a copywriter
who work together. These arrangements are often tem-
porary. Only once in a while does a team form a permanent bond.

De facto teams have often operated at a corporation's upper level. Tom Murphy and Dan Burke have
run Capital Cities/ABC as a team for 18 years. Then
there's Al Checchi and Gary Wilson at Northwest Airlines.

Wilson first met Checchi in 1963, when he took a
job with a Washington, D.C., consulting firm run by

Checchi's uncle. In 1974 Wilson joined Marriott Corp. The following year he hired Checchi. In 1982 Checchi went to work for the Bass Organization in Fort Worth. In 1984 he helped engineer a swap of the Basses' Arvida real estate unit for a 25 percent stake in Walt Disney, then spent six months helping Disney devise a strategic plan. That same year Wilson joined Disney as chief financial officer.

The Disney connection was very rewarding for both Checchi and Wilson. Checchi made a $50 million profit. Wilson made almost $65 million. In 1989 Al Checchi and Gary Wilson put some of those millions, along with a lot of borrowed money, into buying Northwest Airlines for $3.65 billion.

The full potential of business partners has not really been explored. But something magical happens when two people who have mutual trust in each other work together. They tend to be able to run rings around their individual competitors.

Married partners

What happens when business partners are also married to each other? We see this as a definite trend as more women join the the work force, especially in executive positions.

Rather than working at a disadvantage, married partners can form a powerful combination. Assuming the marriage is all right, they have a stronger commitment to each other. They are usually much more open and honest. (The best business partnerships have always been much like a marriage.)

Michael Ruby and Merrill McLoughlin were re-

cently named coeditors of *U.S. News & World Report.*
Nothing unusual about their appointment except that
they have been married for the past three years. "People think highly of them both," says a senior editor at
U.S. News. "They tend to speak remarkably well with
one voice. They also have more than four decades of
combined experience. They're the Ozzie and Harriet of
newsmagazines."

Arthur Ortenberg had been running his own textile
company, and his wife was a fashion designer. They had
been married for 19 years when they decided to launch
a company to clothe the working American woman. "I
was working myself, I wanted to look good, and I didn't
think you should have to spend a fortune to do it," said
his wife.

In 1976 they founded Liz Claiborne Inc. with
$50,000 in savings and $200,000 raised from family
and friends. Thirteen years later, with $1.3 billion in
sales, Liz Claiborne was the second-largest apparel company (after V. F. Corporation) on the *Fortune* 500 list.

Liz Claiborne and her husband Arthur Ortenberg
are prime examples of the power of married partners.
But what happens when the marriage breaks up?

That's the down side of married partners, and there's
no better example than Doug and Susie Tompkins. Like
Ortenberg and Claiborne, the Tompkins cofounded a
fashion firm. Called Esprit de Corp, the venture was a big
success. Worldwide sales in 1989 were more than $1 billion.

Somewhere along the way to building a billion-dollar business, the Tompkins' marriage started to fall
apart. Their personal differences spilled over into the

business. She wanted the company to design clothes for career-oriented women. He wanted the product line to be more whimsical. Each tried to undermine the other's actions by forming rival alliances with employees. Sales and profits plummeted.

After years of turmoil Doug Tompkins agreed to sell his 50 percent stake to an investor group led by his wife Susie Tompkins.

Finding a partner

Attitude is your most important attribute in finding a partner. You have to keep an open mind.

Most people are gregarious in social situations but loners in business ones. They tend to see their fellow employees as competitors, as indeed they are in a typical big-company situation. That attitude spills over into relationships with outsiders. Many big-company people tend to become hard-nosed, demanding, and critical, especially with suppliers.

Before you can find a partner, you have to find a friend. But friendship is not nearly enough if you want to find an effective partner. You have to develop respect for your partner's opinion, even if it differs from your own. For many people this is exceptionally difficult to do. Many people do not respect anyone else's opinion if it differs from theirs. If you have this problem, then you have to start working on yourself before you start working on finding a partner.

Mutual respect is the glue that keeps partners together in good times as well as bad.

11

The Spouse Horse

Let's say your long-term goal is to manage the Plaza Hotel in New York City. You could start by going to Cornell's School of Hotel Administration and Management in Ithaca, New York.

Then perhaps you could find a position in the back offices of Hilton, Westin, or one of the other major hotel chains. If you're lucky, you could work your way up the chain by managing, say, a Radisson in Milwaukee, Wisconsin. Then how do you make your move from Milwaukee to the Big Apple? Not an easy task.

Alternatively, you could marry Donald Trump as Ivana Zelnicek did and wind up at the age of 40 as manager of the Plaza with $50 million to spend on refurbishing.

Suppose, however, your long-term goal is to manage the Helmsley Palace, another Manhattan landmark, a few blocks east of the Plaza. Sorry, but Leona Helmsley got there first.

Marriage used to be for two reasons: love and/or

children. But times are changing. New divorce laws have redefined marriage as an "economic partnership."

In the living room as well as in the courtroom, marriage has been an economic partnership for many years. Most women, like most men, are employed. (Fifty-six percent of all adult women have jobs, compared with 76 percent of the men.)

Furthermore, women with children are more likely to have jobs than women without kids. Sixty-five percent of all married women with children under 18 are employed.

"The man works, the woman stays home and takes care of the kids" is a myth that hasn't been true for many years. No wonder the women of Wellesley College were up in arms over the choice of Barbara Bush as their commencement speaker. She no longer represents a role model for the majority.

When Wellesley graduates commence, they are more likely to do it in the offices of Corporate America than in the kitchens of suburbia.

While women are finding jobs in increasing numbers, what they aren't finding is equal pay. The shocking fact is that women earn substantially less than men. In America today the average female *college* graduate makes less money ($25,544 a year) than the average male *high school* graduate ($27,293 a year).

With both spouses working or looking for work, it's a tragic waste to ignore what you can do for your spouse, or vice versa. There are signs that riding the Spouse Horse is becoming more and more popular. "The people in our set don't marry for richer or poorer," says one power wife. "They marry for richer and richer."

What about love? Who's to say why people marry the people they do. If you marry for money instead of love, at least you suffer in comfort.

For whatever reason you find yourself married, make the most of it. It's a crime not to. No one is likely to be more helpful in your career than your spouse. No one has more motivation to help you. No one is more available 24 hours a day than a spouse.

Every one of us needs someone else to give us a boost up the ladder. We find it ironic that many people would rather ask a stranger for help than their own spouse. An "economic partnership" implies cooperation, not competition. What can your spouse do for you? Here are five obvious things.

1. Money

Obviously, marrying money is a lot quicker than earning money. But the trick isn't to live off the money. Your real objective should be to build something bigger with your new financial base. Something you can point to as yours just in case things get a little rocky in the marriage. Making the transition from your spouse's money to your own money is tricky, but not impossible.

Georgette Mosbacher is making the transition. Called "nervy, sexy, flashy, and filthy rich," by the *Washington Post Magazine,* she married her third husband, Commerce Secretary Robert Mosbacher, in 1985. Three years later, Ms. Mosbacher bought La Prairie, a Swiss cosmetics firm, for $31.5 million.

Where did she get the money? From everyone. Venture capitalists, banks, La Prairie distributors in Switzerland and Japan. She also tapped her own and her husband's resources.

So far, so good. In the first year under Georgette Mosbacher's control, La Prairie's sales were up 30 percent.

Carolyne Roehm is one of New York City's most successful young designers. At the age of 33, she opened her own design firm by renting half a floor in the same Seventh Avenue building that housed Ralph Lauren, Geoffrey Beene, and Bill Blass. Seven months later Roehm unveiled her first collection of elegant evening wear and sprightly day wear. The show was a smashing success.

Who put up the several million dollars that Roehm needed to start her design firm? The leveraged buyout king Henry Kravis, whose fortune today is estimated at $400 million. Shortly thereafter, Carolyne Roehm and Henry Kravis were married.

Why not? If you think enough of a person to want to marry them, why not put money into your spouse-to-be's business? You can't divorce love and money.

Andrea Jovine, a 25-year-old graduate of Fashion Institute of Technology, had a small accessories firm when she was introduced to Victor Coopersmith. The former head of an apparel firm, Coopersmith was looking to start up a new company.

Not only did Mr. Coopersmith end up financing Ms. Jovine's apparel business; he fell in love with her. In 1989 they were married.

In the meantime, Andrea Jovine, now 33 years old, has become a phenomenon among working women fed up with the dressed-for-success look. She offers them the alternative of snug-fitting knits, a look that's rapidly taking over at major department stores. Sales of Andrea Jovine fashions are currently in the neighborhood of $50 million. Not a bad neighborhood.

Sometimes an ex-spouse is an even better source of money than a current one. Frances Lear arrived in New York in 1985 at the age of 61. Freshly divorced from her television producer/husband, Norman (*All in the Family*) Lear, she determined to launch a magazine for women over 40. She was prepared to spend $25 million of her expected $112 million settlement on the project.

By its fifth issue, *Lear's Magazine* had 350,000 readers. "I haven't seen a start-up like this in my career," says Kevin Gruneich, publishing analyst at First Boston Corp. "Lear is on her way to having a very successful magazine. The time it took her to get where she is is just unbelievably short."

Every business, especially in the beginning, needs money. The best place to look for it is at home. Yet some people hesitate to ask their spouses for help. They feel it's not quite right; they want to be financially independent. That's nonsense. Don't marry a rich person if you don't want to ride the Spouse Horse.

Almost no one makes it on his own anyway. It's no disgrace to reach for help outside of yourself. If there's a horse in your house, ride it.

2. Connections

Sometimes money is not the issue. What you really need are connections. A spouse who can open doors can be enormously helpful in building a business.

Linda Robinson, the wife of Jim Robinson (CEO of American Express), is president of Robinson, Lake, Lerer & Montgomery, a successful public relations firm. Among her major clients are Commercial Credit Group (Chairman Sandy Weill is the former president of American Express) and Squibb (CEO Richard Furland is a director of American Express). Her friends include Tom Brokaw, Diane Sawyer, Barbara Walters, and Henry Kravis. Kravis joined her in buying a race horse.

In a front-page profile of Linda Robinson in 1988, *The Wall Street Journal* said, "At 35 she appears poised to wield a degree of behind-the-scenes influence approaching that of a few superlawyers and image makers."

3. Encouragement

Sometimes the best thing one spouse can do for the other is provide a healthy dose of encouragement.

Adrienne Toth gave up a budding fashion career when she married Italian pharmaceutical heir Gianluigi Vittadini in 1972 and went to live in Italy. Six years later, when her husband's business took him to New York, he pushed her to start her own company.

"He was not at all involved in the fashion industry at that time," says Adrienne Vittadini. "But he helped set up my company. It could never have been so successful without him. He gave me the confidence and the vision." A few years later Mr. Vittadini joined the company full-time. Today Adrienne Vittadini, their booming fashion business, is a $150 million-a-year business. Adrienne is chairman and her husband, Gianluigi, is vice chairman.

4. Family

Sometimes it's not the spouse who has the money or the connections; it's the spouse's family. The classic example, of course, is marrying the boss's daughter and then taking over the company. Don't think this is something that happens only at small, insignificant companies.

Edwin C. "Skip" Gage 3d married Barbara Carlson, daughter of Curt Carlson, founder of Carlson Companies in Minneapolis, a conglomerate that has more than $5 billion in annual sales.

After a stint with a Chicago advertising agency, Skip Gage joined the company in 1969. He became president in 1984 and is currently being groomed to become chief executive of Carlson, the nation's fifteenth largest private enterprise.

5. Inheritance

Unfortunately some people get to ride the Spouse Horse only after the death of their spouse.

Mary Roebling was a young widow in 1937 when she inherited control of the Trenton Trust Company from her late husband Siegfried Roebling. She proceeded to pioneer an outstanding business career: first woman chairman of a major U.S. bank, first woman governor of the American Stock Exchange, chairman of the Women's Bank of Denver. In 1990 she was named USO's Woman of the Year.

Gertrude Crain is chairman of Crain Communications Inc., a publishing powerhouse. Founded by G. D. Crain, Jr., the company now owns 25 business publications and takes in about $140 million a year. Her two sons — Rance, president, and Keith, vice chairman — run the newspapers and magazines, but Gertrude Crain handles the money.

How she became involved with Crain finances is a story in itself. One day when her sons were in high school, she went downtown to G. D. Crain's office and asked him, "What are we doing with all this money that we're making?"

He suggested that she take charge of investing it. Her first reaction was, "My God, this man must be out of his mind." But she learned the Wall Street ropes soon enough, and still manages the family's capital, plus the company's pension, benefit, and profit-sharing funds.

After her husband's death, Gertrude Crain positioned herself squarely at the center of things by taking charge of accounts payable. At the age of 79, she signs every nonpayroll check that Crain issues. (Why retire if you're having fun?)

Corazon Aquino is another woman who took over after her husband's death. While it's no fun being President of the Philippines these days, her courageous story is an example of how, even after your spouse's death, you can still ride the Spouse Horse.

12

The Family Horse

Do you believe that success is just a matter of talent? Most people do, especially those who have already made it to the top.

There's something intellectually satisfying about believing in meritocracy. Those who made it did so because of merit. Those who didn't ... well, we can't all be smart or brilliant or talented.

A little study of the situation shows that the differences between abilities are not nearly so great as the differences between accomplishments. Why is it that some people are extraordinarily successful and others are not? If you look at business, for example, one reason is the family connection.

Instead of a meritocracy, we live in a clanocracy. When a recent college graduate was asked how he got his high-paying position, he said he went to see the chief executive of the biggest company in town and asked, "Dad, how about a job?"

More and more, the future belongs to the family firm. There are 15 million businesses in America, and almost 90 percent are family-controlled or have a major family involvement. They employ 45 million people and generate 60 percent of our gross national product.

Many of these are mom-and-pop operations, to be sure, but an awful lot of giant corporations are also family-controlled. Anheuser-Busch, Seagram's, Mars, Estée Lauder, Marriott, to name a few. Family ownership is significant in about 175 of the *Fortune* 500, including the second-largest company in the world, Ford Motor.

Any way you slice it, the family accounts for a substantial share of the business pie.

More than 31,000 family-held businesses have annual sales of more than $25 million. Sole proprietorships and partnerships earn 18 percent of U.S. business income—some $580 billion.

The Family Horse ought to be your first choice. Before you look for another horse to ride, look at your birth certificate. If you find a name like Bronfman, Busch, Crain, Ford, Kennedy, Lauder, Marriott, Mars, Newhouse, Sulzberger, Tisch, or Trump, look no further. These are powerful family dynasties. Maybe your family belongs on this list. If so, accept your good fortune. Don't fight it. A horse in the house is worth two in the fields.

Too many family scions, however, want to do it on their own. For ego reasons or perhaps out of a sense of fairness, they don't want to ride the Family Horse. "I'm terrific. I did it on my own" is what they want to be able to say. So they walk away from the family.

If you are thinking along the same lines, let us give you some advice. Nobody makes it on his own. Everybody needs a horse to ride. You'll never honestly be able to say, "I did it all by myself" anyway, so you might as well ride the horse you were born with.

The real tragedy is not that the children don't have horse sense. The real tragedy is when the parents don't. They want to have their cake and eat it too. They want to bring their offspring into the family business and then promote them on merit only.

That's a mistake. Everybody needs a horse to ride. If you are the parent, would you deny your son or daughter the same opportunity? Either you let them ride the Family Horse, along with all the advantages that implies, or you throw them out and force them to look for a totally different horse.

Parents, in particular, need to develop their horse sense. They can be thoughtlessly cruel when they hold their sons or daughters to the same standards as they do their other employees. The English media tycoon Robert Maxwell once fired his own son for forgetting to pick him up at the airport.

It's not easy to ride the Family Horse, but it can be profitable. The richest family in America, worth $12.5 billion, owns Mars Inc., the candy company that controls 37 percent of the U.S. market. Mars brands include Snickers (the largest-selling candy bar), Milky Way, and M&Ms.

The company is now run by copresidents Forrest Mars, Jr., and John Mars, sons of the chairman and grandsons of the founder. Fourth-generation Mars children are starting to work for the company.

The same pattern was repeated at White Castle Systems. Founded by E. W. "Billy" Ingram in 1921, White Castle is now run by chairman E. W. "Edgar" Ingram II and president E. W. "Bill" Ingram III.

"Where else," said Bill Ingram, "could I be president of a $282 million business at the age of 37?" Actually Bill Ingram took over the White Castle chief executive position at the tender age of 28. Not a bad job if you can get it.

Tony George was just 30 when he became president of the Indianapolis Motor Speedway. Tony is the only grandson of the late Tony Hulman, who bought the track in 1945. The Speedway's board is a family affair. It includes his mother, board chairman Mari Hulman George, and his two sisters.

Bill Killebrew was just 23 when he became president and managing general partner of Heavenly Ski Area, the nation's biggest resort, with 12,800 skiable acres and the world's largest snowmaking system. (His father Hugh, the majority owner, died in an accident.)

A family doesn't have to own a company to control it. The Watson family never owned more than a few percent of the shares of IBM. Yet they controlled the company for 57 years. Their problem was knowing when to let go.

Tom Watson, Sr., was 82 years old, and had only six weeks to live, before he turned the reins of IBM over to his son Tom Watson, Jr. Before that happened, the two had many bitter arguments. "It amazes me," said Tom Jr., "that two people could torture each other to the degree Dad and I did and not call it quits."

Nor was Tom Jr. sensitive to the needs and wants of his younger brother Dick. Instead of setting him up as the heir apparent, he put Dick in a senseless competition. "I thought I was being scrupulously fair," said Tom Watson, Jr., "but in hindsight it was the worst business and family mistake I ever made. I should never have forced my brother into a horse race with other executives for the top job."

Right. Fairness has nothing to do with it. Family Horse owners beware. When you treat your son or daughter just like another employee, you're breaking the unwritten code. Family is family. Oddly enough, your other employees know how the game is played. They would treat their own family as family, so why should you do otherwise? (Dick Watson resigned from IBM to become ambassador to France.)

Why do some dynasties hold onto the illusion that ability counts more than family? They are fooling no one but themselves.

Learning to share power

Laurence and Preston Tisch are sons of Al Tisch, the entrepreneur who started the conglomerate that became Loews Corporation. In addition to hotels and theaters, Loews owns a tobacco company (Lorillard), an insurance company (CNA), and a watch company (Bulova). Today the two Tisches, according to *Forbes* magazine, are worth $2.7 billion.

The Tisches have learned what the Watsons never did: how to share power. Laurence, the older brother, is chairman. Preston is president. They share the CEO title. (Laurence is also CEO of CBS Inc., the television network. His election followed Loews' purchase of a substantial share of CBS stock.)

Tisch offspring are also well positioned in the Loews hierarchy. Laurence's son James is executive vice president of Loews Corporation. His son Andrew recently moved from president of Bulova to chairman of

Lorillard. Preston's son Jonathan is president of Loews Hotels.

Si and Donald Newhouse also smoothly share the power at the Newhouse family company, Advance Publications. Si runs the books and magazines. Donald runs the newspapers.

Founded by their father, Samuel Newhouse, Advance is no lightweight publisher. Advance owns Random House, 26 newspapers, and more than a dozen magazines, including *The New Yorker, Vogue, Vanity Fair,* and *Glamour.* This package of properties has made the Newhouse clan the second-richest family in America.

Like the Newhouses, the second-generation Crains have learned how to divide the power at Crain Communications. Rance runs half the company from the deck of his flagship publication *Advertising Age.* Keith runs the other half from his flagship *Automotive News.* The two sides of the company have little to do with each other. "All of Crain," as the saying goes in the ranks, "is divided in twain."

Even a large family can learn how to share the power. Five sons and daughters of William T. Dillard are working together at Dillard Department Stores, the company founded by their father. Bill is president, Alex and Mike are executive vice presidents, Drue is vice president of merchandising, and Denise is a divisional merchandise manager. (What happens when chairman William T. Dillard retires is another matter.)

Malcolm Forbes gave each of his five children an equal financial share of his estate. But he solved the succession problem by giving his eldest son Steve, who had been president and deputy editor in chief of *Forbes* magazine, 51 percent control. Should the eldest son or daughter be the one who inherits control of a family firm?

Probably. It may not be fair, but at least it's simple and easy to remember. Very early in their careers all members of the family know on whose shoulders the mantle will fall.

You don't need majority control to ride the Family Horse. Both William C. Ford, Jr., and Edsel B. Ford II are working their way up the ladder at Ford. Billy is 33 and Edsel is 41. Both are on the board of directors and both have indicated they want to either run the family company or have a top management role. (The family controls 40 percent of Ford's voting stock.)

If you have the opportunity, you might as well ride the Family Horse when you can. Face the facts, however. It's probably impossible for a family to ride one horse forever. The penalty of success is often an influx of outside financing, a listing on the New York Stock Exchange, and eventually loss of control.

A Rockwell had been head of Rockwell International for more than 50 years, but the family didn't continue its leadership into the third generation. (It wasn't for a lack of riders. William F. Rockwell, Jr., had five children.)

Nor did the Watsons keep control of IBM. Success is a two-edged sword. It can make a family extremely wealthy at the same time that it knocks it off the horse.

When the family feuds

No feud can be as bitter and as violent as a family feud.

Leonard Shoen, founder of U-Haul, started transferring stock to his children while they were still young.

Trouble was, Shoen had eight sons and five daughters. Ultimately he gave away 95 percent of U-Haul, which had grown into Amerco with revenues of about $1 billion.

In 1986 two of Shoen's sons, Edward and Mark, seized control and voted the senior Shoen out. Soon afterward, Sam, the eldest son, quit.

The family has split into two camps. Edward and Mark are running the show, while Leonard and Sam are suing to regain control. The battle has gotten violent. Stockholder meetings have degenerated into slugfests.

"I created a monster," says dad.

Some feuds are never settled. In 1924 Adi Dassler and his brother Rudolph started a sporting goods company in Germany called Adidas. In 1948 they broke up after a bitter battle. Rudolph set up Puma and the two brothers never spoke to each other again.

Today Adidas is the world's second-biggest sporting goods company. (Puma is also doing quite well.) But the feud continues. The two sides of the Dassler family still avoid each other. The feud extends to the work force. Adidas employees seldom socialize with Puma workers.

Riding the Family Horse is easier if you have a little tolerance. How would you like to be working for your mother ... at the age of 57? Leonard Lauder seems to like it. Of course, his mother is Estée Lauder, the last of the great American cosmetic queens.

Estée Lauder is a family business in every sense of the word. Started by Joseph and Estée in 1946, the company has made the Lauders a family of billionaires. Today even Leonard's wife Eleanor works for the cosmetics concern. The one who is left out is Leonard's younger brother, Ronald.

Working for your mother is apparently not as difficult as working with your brother. Leonard Lauder admits they had problems. "It was my show," says Leonard. After 17 years with Estée Lauder, Ronald quit the company.

It's not impossible for siblings to work together, even in the fashion business. The four Benetton siblings — Giuliana, Luciano, Gilberto, and Carlo — seem to work well together in their Italian retail clothing chain. Maybe it's because the financial incentive is so large. Together they are worth at least $1.7 billion. Separately, who knows?

The Benettons are the exception. Sibling rivalry can be vicious. Certainly it seems to be more common and more serious than generational disputes, although there are plenty of father/son, mother/daughter, father/daughter, and mother/son arguments. Sibling rivalry in the second generation or cousin competition in the third generation has unhorsed many family corporations. The third-generation squabbling of the Gettys resulted in the sale of Getty Petroleum Corp. The same thing happened to the Richardsons and Richardson-Vicks Inc.

Also the Binghams, who were involved in a particularly nasty fight before they sold the family jewel, the *Louisville Courier Journal*.

Campbell Soup Company is headed in the same direction. Founded by Dr. J. T. Dorrance, the chemist who invented condensed soup, the company survived the second generation with J. T. Dorrance, Jr., at the helm. It's the third generation that can't agree on what to do with Campbell Soup. The three children of J. T. Jr., who control 32 percent of the shares, want the company to remain independent. Their six cousins, who own 27 percent, want to sell it. Whatever happens, it's likely that the Dorrances will lose control of Campbell.

No one is suffering. Each of the three Dorrances earn more than $13 million a year from their soup stock.

Sibling rivalry recently flared up at Syms, a $300 million-a-year discount clothing company. When founder and chairman Sy Syms named his daughter Marcy president, two of her three brothers promptly left the company. (One did return, however.)

Building a family dynasty

William Osgood Taylor is the fourth-generation Taylor to head the 117-year-old Affiliated Publications and its flagship newspaper, the *Boston Globe*. The dynasty was started in 1872 by General Charles Taylor along with financier Eben Jordan. Today some 160 members of the Taylor and Jordan clans control the company. Their combined fortune is estimated at $1.75 billion.

Waiting in the wings for his turn on stage is Ben Taylor, executive editor of the *Globe*. He would be the fifth Taylor to run the company.

Waiting in the wings at *The New York Times* is Arthur Ochs (Pinch) Sulzberger, Jr., son of the publisher, Arthur Ochs (Punch) Sulzberger.

Pinch's great grandfather, Adolph Ochs, was a Tennessee newsman who bought the *Times* in 1896 for $75,000. His son-in-law, Arthur Hays Sulzberger, took over in 1935 and ran the paper until 1961. Then he turned the reins over to his own son-in-law, Orvil

Dryfoos, the husband of his eldest daughter, Marian. (Marrying the boss's daughter used to be a sure path to the top. Today, however, the boss's daughter is likely to want the job for herself.)

Dryfoos died two years later, so Sulzberger then turned to his son Punch. At the age of 36, Punch suddenly became the boss of people who were much older and more experienced than he was. Like many other family members who found themselves in similar positions, Punch Sulzberger handled the job well. Talent is only a minor aspect of managing a company. It's hard to go wrong when you have the right name, the right position, and the authority to go along with it.

Money makes money. At last count, The New York Times Company owned 27 daily and 9 weekly newspapers, 17 magazines (including *Family Circle* and *McCall's*), five television stations, and assorted other properties. The family trusts control stock worth $550 million. In addition, members of the Sulzberger family have substantial stock holdings outside the trusts.

The clock is ticking. Punch is now 64 and Pinch is 37, so presumably Pinch's turn at bat will come soon.

Anheuser-Busch is another American institution still under family control. The current chief executive officer, August Busch III, is the fourth-generation Busch to serve the company in that capacity. His great grandfather, Adolphus Busch, started the dynasty by marrying Eberhard Anheuser's daughter. Adolphus joined his father-in-law's brewery as a salesman, later becoming a partner and finally president of the company.

Anheuser-Busch is a marketing powerhouse, with sales approaching $10 billion a year. (Budweiser alone is a $5 billion-a-year brand.) Yet its leader dropped out of the University of Arizona after only two years. August Busch III was best known as a jet-setting playboy with a special affection for skiing and fishing.

He also had the perfect last name for running a beer company. So who will inherit the CEO position when August III retires? Our bet is on his eldest son, August IV.

In theory, nepotism might be a bad idea for a public company like Anheuser-Busch, with 47,000 employees. In practice, however, we see little difference in management ability between family executives and nonfamily executives.

Actually, August Busch III has done a superb job, earning the $8,861,000 he was paid last year. In the last decade, Anheuser-Busch has increased its share of the U.S. beer market from 28 to 43 percent, a gain of 15 percent. Compare his performance with that of Roger Smith, who was then chief impresario of General Motors. Over roughly the same period of time, GM lost 10 percent of the U.S. car market.

Edgar Bronfman, Jr., will also be a third generation family member to head an alcoholic beverage company. He moved up the ladder fast, getting the Seagram president's job at the age of 34, seven years after joining the company. Not bad for a young man who passed up college and plunged into the world of show business when he was 16 years old. Even more surprising is that Edgar was chosen over his older brother, Sam, who did go to college before joining Seagram. (Sam now runs Seagram's domestic wine business and shows no apparent resentment toward his younger brother, Edgar.)

Complicating the succession problem at Seagram is

the fact that Edgar's father, Edgar Bronfman, Sr., has a brother Charles, who is cochairman of Seagram. Furthermore, Charles has a son and daughter who might also have been interested in running Seagram.

The Bronfman clan has shown remarkable agility in keeping the House of Seagram in the family. Whether they can weather the storms into the fourth generation remains to be seen. Certainly the stakes are worthwhile. The Bronfmans' 38 percent share of Seagram is worth more than $2 billion.

Ability is not the issue. Anybody with a three-digit IQ and reasonable diplomatic skills can run a modern corporation in a lackluster way, indistinguishable from the top managers of most other big companies. Ego, greed, and jealousy are what determines the issue. Too much of these qualities and the family-controlled firm dissolves in a cloud of intramural warfare.

When the generations do work together, the Family Horse can be exceptionally powerful. Barney's was a small discount men's clothing store started three generations ago by Barney Pressman. Today Barney's is one of the bright lights of the New York retail scene, doing about $100 million a year in men's and women's clothing at one location in Manhattan. Barney's has become an American institution, a development that didn't happen overnight. Forty-year-old Gene Pressman runs the company along with his brother Robert.

Bill Marriott got his start when his father opened the Hot Shoppe, a nine-seat root-beer stand in Washington, D.C., in 1927. Today the Marriott Corp. is an $8 billion company with 230,000 people on the payroll. Marriott owns 558 hotels as well as Howard Johnson,

Big Boy Restaurants, and airport gift shops. The family's stock is worth at least $1.4 billion.

Bill Marriott was even younger than Edgar Bronfman when Marriott Sr. turned the company over to him. Although a public company, Marriott is firmly under family control. Bill's brother Richard is vice chairman. Together with their mother, the Marriotts hold three of the eight seats on the board.

Passing the baton to the next generation might be a problem. Two of Bill Marriott's three sons (ages 29 and 31) and his son in law are employed by the company, but none is high on the executive ladder. "The question is," says Marriott, "do they want to sit in this office? They'll have to show that they're energetic, bright, dedicated, and committed."

Hmm. Sounds like Bill Marriott forgot how he and his brother made it to the top.

A Family Horse helps you get off to a good start. And getting a good start is at least half the battle. Robert Haft was only 24 years old and just four months out of Harvard Business School when he started Crown Books, the nation's first deep-discount retail book chain.

Haft had lots of help. His father, Herbert Haft, started Dart, the first discount drugstore chain. (Angry competitors cried "unfair trade" and sued but lost in Supreme Court.) When existing malls prohibited Dart from leasing space, he developed his own shopping centers under the Combined Properties name.

In the beginning, Crown rented space in buildings owned or leased by Combined Properties. (When you're trying to get a retail business off the ground, it's helpful to have Dad as your landlord.) Robert Haft opened his first store in Rockville, Maryland, in 1977. Today Crown has 257 bookstores across the country. Revenues exceed $200 million a year.

The Haft dynasty also includes Robert's brother Ronald (age 30), who runs Combined Properties, and his sister Linda (age 38), who is executive vice president of the family's financial arm. The Haft family fortune is estimated at over $400 million.

You don't have to own the entire horse in order to ride it. Akio Morita became famous as the founder of Sony, but he and his family own only 10 percent of the stock. It was enough to allow his brother, Masaaki Morita, to become one of Sony's two deputy presidents.

Many family dynasties are a family affair in a real sense of the word. In the winter of 1952, Dave McCoy was a full-time hydrographer for the city of Los Angeles. His Monday-to-Friday job was measuring the Sierra snowpack. On weekends, he ran his own business, setting up portable tows on slopes in the Mammoth region. His wife Roma collected the $2 lift fee.

Today Dave McCoy is owner of the twin California resorts of Mammoth Mountain and June Mountain. (Mammoth sells more lift tickets per year than any other ski area in the Western Hemisphere.) His entire family is involved in the operation, which includes a 216-room hotel, three lodges, four ski slopes, three cafeterias, and two restaurants.

Gary, the eldest of six children, is Mammoth's general manager. Kandi manages the smaller June Mountain complex. Penny is coordinator of special events. Randy is the company pilot. Carl runs a ranch in British

Columbia that supplies beef cattle for Mammoth and June. So does Dennis, who owns a ranch in Montana.

The McCoys are an example of how a large family can work together harmoniously. Not every family dynasty, however, has a good track record in this regard.

The Dodge brothers, John and Horace, introduced the Dodge automobile in 1914. Six years later, they were selling 150,000 cars a year, second only to Ford. Their joint fortune was around $200 million, the equivalent of about $1.5 billion today.

Then, suddenly, both brothers were dead. John died early in 1920, Horace a few months later. Both men were in their fifties and left their wives, ex-wives, and eight children their immense fortune. Unfortunately, none of the heirs knew the first thing about handling their wealth. Nor did they know the first thing about the nature of work.

Horace Dodge, Jr., once tried working on the factory floor for a few weeks, but as he explained to the press, his hardest job was getting up at 6 a.m. His mother encouraged this attitude. She wanted her son to conquer high society, not spend his life in a hot and greasy machine shop like his father. With no work and no responsibilities, the Dodge heirs were devoted to high living and to suing one another for more money. Throughout the twenties, the Dodge debacles were covered almost daily in the press: financial problems, divorces, custody battles, speeding tickets, even jail sentences.

The Family Horse is not about money itself or even the things that money can buy, but the opportunity that money represents. The opportunity to use your family connection to build a position of power and responsibility and, most important of all, self-respect.

Like the Dodges, some families squander their opportunities in squabbles and careless living. Cornelius Vanderbilt was once the world's richest person. When he died in 1877, he left his heirs an estate larger than the United States Treasury. Yet within 70 years of his death, the last of the great Vanderbilt mansions that once lined Manhattan's Fifth Avenue had been broken to rubble. When 120 of his descendants gathered at Vanderbilt University in 1973 for the first family reunion, there wasn't a millionaire left among them.

Women riders

It's become a frustrating decade for women who want a career, especially for those who want to get into the upper ranks of corporate management. Only one woman heads a company listed in the *Fortune* 500 directory. She is Katherine Graham, chairman of the Washington Post Company (owner of the newspaper of the same name as well as *Newsweek* magazine and four television stations.) Ms. Graham did not start at the bottom and work her way up the ladder. (No matter how talented a woman might be, that's not possible in today's sexist environment. And the larger the company, the more impossible it becomes for a woman to reach the top by ability alone.)

Katherine Graham rode the Family Horse to the top of the 269th largest U.S. industrial company. The job originally belonged to her father, Eugene Meyer, who bought the newspaper at auction in 1933, at the bottom of the Depression. When he became president of the World Bank in 1946, Meyer turned the *Post* over to his daughter and her husband, Philip Graham. It wasn't until Philip's death 15 years later that sole responsibility for the company fell into Katherine's hands.

Women have a tough time getting to the top. Recently *Fortune* magazine examined the proxy statements of the public companies on its combined list of the 1000 largest U.S. industrial and service companies. Of the 4012 highest-paid officers and directors, only 19 were women. That's less than one-half of 1 percent.

When *Fortune* did a similar study of 6400 officers and directors in 1978, it found 10 women. So you can say women have made progress. In 12 years, the percentage of women in the top corporate jobs increased 200 percent. But women are still outnumbered by men 211 to 1. Women have come from nowhere to almost nowhere.

Nor is the situation likely to change in the near future. "My generation came out of graduate school 15 or 20 years ago," says a 46-year old woman executive. "The men are now next in line to run major corporations. The women are not. Period."

As you know by now, we are dubious about your chances for success aboard the Company Horse. That's if you are a man. If you are a woman, we are doubly dubious about your odds.

The Family Horse is a much better bet. Assuming, of course, that you selected the right parents, you can have a superb ride on this horse. It's an almost certain ticket to the top.

Bernadette Castro is president of Castro Convertibles Corporation, a highly successful furniture manu-

facturer and retailer. Founded by her mother and father in a loft in New York City, the company made
Bernadette famous by starring her in television commercials in the fifties. (The corporate logo still depicts
her as a little girl opening a Castro convertible.)

Perhaps the best-known woman executive in the
New York area, Bernadette Castro has it all. A $200-
million company, a 30-room mansion on the Long Island Sound, a 108-foot yacht, not to mention four children and a husband, Dr. Peter Guida. (Eat your heart
out, Donald Trump.)

Christie Hefner is another example. As unlikely as it
might seem, Ms. Hefner became president of Playboy
Enterprises, publishers of *Playboy* magazine, at the early
age of 29. (She was younger than some of the center-
folds.) Her father, Hugh Hefner, owns 70 percent of
the company, as you might expect.

What you might not expect is that Ms. Hefner has
done a credible job at Playboy in a difficult environment. In 1984 she was named chief operating officer.
In 1989, chief executive. With $166 million in annual
revenues, Playboy is a substantial company with a lot of
potential. Christie Hefner has many more years to
build Playboy into a publishing powerhouse like the
Washington Post. She's only 36.

While it's obvious that women can do everything
that men can do, it's not always obvious how to get into
the game. At the wild and woolly Comex (Manhattan's
Commodities Exchange), there are only a handful of
women. One of these is 37-year-old Donna Redel, executive vice president of Redel Trading Corp.

Nearly a decade ago, her father asked her to join
the family's commodities firm. She did and helped turn

Redel Trading into one of the dominant companies on the floor of the Comex. She has earned enough respect from her peers to have been elected chairman (an anachronism) of the exchange's operations committee, a key oversight group. She also sits on the Comex's board of directors.

Why don't more daughters do what Donna Redel did? We asked that question of Carrie Schwab Pomerantz, daughter of Charles Schwab, the fabulously successful founder of the first discount brokerage firm. "Actually, I did go to work for Charles Schwab," she said. "I took the training and became a licensed stock broker." Then she left to get married and to join Burroughs-Wellcome, the pharmaceutical company that produces AZT, where she holds a key marketing position.

Why doesn't Carrie Schwab work for Charles Schwab? "I wanted to be successful on my own," she states, "not just the boss's daughter." That's a psychologically sound attitude, probably good for one's mental health, and a widely held belief among the sons and daughters of the rich and famous.

Which is one reason we wrote this book. You can't be successful totally on your own. Everyone needs a horse to ride. Why not ride the one you were born with?

If you're a parent, give your offspring more than just a starting job with the family firm. Give them encouragement. Give them understanding. "I know you want to be successful on your own, but everybody needs a horse to ride. And I'm your horse, so hop on."

Be honest. You might even share with them the inside story of how you got your fancy title and your name on the door. In other words, the name of the horse that got you started on the road to success. It's probably someone or something you have been keeping under wraps all these years because "you wanted to be successful on your own."

That's especially true if you have a daughter. Many parents push their sons but not their daughters. Katharine Graham made her son Donald publisher of the *Washington Post*, not Elizabeth, Donald's older sister. Why not?

Arthur Cinadar asked his daughter Emily to join his company, J. Crew Group, after she graduated from the University of Denver in the early eighties. Since then J. Crew has struck gold. Since mailing its first catalog in 1983, the company has seen its annual sales skyrocket. The J. Crew style has become almost as much of a yuppie status symbol as Ralph Lauren's Polo, Perrier, BMWs, and frozen yogurt in a waffle cone. J. Crew Group sales in 1989 were about $300 million.

Emily Cinadar is president and design director of J. Crew. She's also just 28 years old. Where else can you get to be president of a $300 million company before turning 30?

Critics might say she only got the job because of her father. True, but so what? Everyone needs a horse to ride, if only an accidental one of happening to be in the right place at the right time.

Critics might say that when her father moves on (he's 62), J. Crew might collapse around her. Probably not true. Actually, the track record of an executive trained by a parent is quite good, usually better than the track record of the stranger hired off the street.

Exploiting the family name

In product marketing, a brand name is powerful, and often essential to a product's success. In people marketing, this principle is usually forgotten.

If you are born with a brand name, take advantage of it. You don't think that Nelson Rockefeller got to be governor of New York and John D. Rockefeller got to be governor of West Virginia purely because they were good politicians. They were given a powerful assist by their well-recognized family brand name.

One of the powerful brand names in New York radio is Gambling. The dynasty was started by John B. Gambling in 1924 on radio station WOR. The morning radio program "Rambling With Gambling" was handed over to his son, John A. Gambling, in 1959. Currently the third generation, John R. Gambling, is in the process of taking over the popular morning show.

Not only have the three Gamblings built a powerful brand name, but also they have made "Rambling With Gambling" the longest-running radio program in America.

The same phenomenon is taking place in television and motion pictures. The Fonda dynasty, for example, was started by veteran actor Henry Fonda with such movies as *12 Angry Men*. His son Peter captured the mood of the rebellious sixties with the classic film *Easy Rider*. His daughter Jane became the family's biggest star with a string of hit movies as well as a wildly successful series of exercise videos. (Even a trip to Hanoi couldn't kill Jane Fonda's rising star.)

In addition to a long line of popular movies and

television shows, Lloyd Bridges produced two sons, Beau and Jeff, who have also become movie actors. *The Fabulous Baker Boys* starred the Bridges brothers.

Three generations of Hustons (Walter, John, and Anjelica) have won Oscars. Then there's Tony Curtis and his daughter Jamie Lee Curtis. John Carradine and his sons David, Keith, and Robert. Martin Sheen and son Charlie. Kirk Douglas and son Michael.

The popular explanation for movie dynasties is that talent is inherited. Maybe. What's just as important is that the brand name is inherited. You can't be a movie star until you get a part in a picture. And it's a lot easier to get a part in a picture if you have a brand name.

What's true in Hollywood is true everywhere else. Most people fail to become movie stars, television stars, radio stars, or even chief executives, not because they don't have the talent but because they don't have the opportunity. Getting into the game is at least three-quarters of the formula for future success.

13

Changing horses

Time runs in the reverse order of the way it should. We should all be born old and experienced and then, as time goes on, we should get younger and younger until one day we disappear into the womb.

That way we would know exactly how to live our lives. Decisions would be easy to make. Hindsight would become foresight.

As odd as it might seem, people do make decisions as if time ran backward. They plan the future with airy confidence that time will unfold exactly as planned. "I'm planning to go to college and then to medical school. After my internship, I'll get married. Then we'll buy a home and have two kids (a boy and a girl.) We'll take up golf and tennis and join a country club. We'll even buy a place in Florida we can retire to some day."

Variations of this scenario no doubt exist in your own mind. Whatever the specific details of your personal scenario, it probably is one continuous line, always going onward and upward. Nowhere in most scenarios are there jagged drops in the lifeline corresponding to such things as getting fired, having your employer go bankrupt, losing your health, and divorcing your spouse. Nor, for that matter, are there sudden rises in the lifeline corresponding to things like winning the lottery, discovering a marvelous invention, or meeting a person who could change your life. In other words, the typical scenario does not include finding a horse to ride.

One reason is that a horse requires change. You may have to change careers, move to another state, take up a different lifestyle. And who wants change?

Practically no one. Of course, everyone wants to do a little better, make a little more money, buy a slightly better house, and buy a more expensive, but not too much more expensive, car. Keep that lifeline moving upward in a smooth and predictable way.

But change—and often a jarring change—is exactly what's usually needed to become a big success in life. When you find the horse, you have to be mentally prepared to ride it. Otherwise, it's just another idle dream. If you always do what you've always done, you will only get what you've always got.

If you have the least bit of ambition, that ought not to be good enough for you. Most people never come close to their real potential. Not for lack of trying and sometimes not even for an inability to find a horse to ride. Most people never come close to their real potential because they are afraid of change. *If you always do what you've always done, you will only get what you've always got.*

You have to force yourself to break the pattern. You have to give up the comfort of the familiar and be willing to put up with the stress of the unfamiliar. Some people have no choice. These are the failures: the people who, for one reason or another, are out of a job. Maybe their company went belly up. Maybe they got fired. Maybe it was their fault. Maybe not.

There are a lot of failures walking the streets. Roughly half of all employees will be fired one or more times during the course of their careers. If this happens to you, take heart.

A higher percentage of "failures" will turn out to be hugely successful than will an equal number of people who never had to go through the ignominy of being laid off. Being fired forces you to make a fresh start. So you look around for an opportunity and maybe you see a horse you can ride.

When you have a job, you tend to stop looking. You tend to focus all of your efforts on your position, your company, your chances for promotion. Your strategy is to work hard and maybe "they" will notice you. You are a horse with the blinders on. Your mind is focused on winning the race.

Some people spend 20 or 30 years running on the same track with very little success. So what do they do? They try harder. We call this the "back of the pack" psychology. (Avis is only No. 2 in rent-a-cars. So why go with us? We try harder.) Hard work clouds the mind and keeps you in the same old rut.

In case you haven't noticed, Avis is still No. 2 and still trying harder. If it doesn't come easy, it probably won't come at all.

Maybe your better strategy is to change horses. Making the decision to change horses is often the hardest part. Finding another horse is often easier.

When should you change horses? Perhaps the oldest

cliché in the employment guidance field is that you should look for a job when your old job isn't fun anymore.

If this is your situation, you have a serious problem. You should have been long gone before your job turned into a terminal case of acute boredom. You're not alone. Procrastination is common among many, many people. They know they should leave, they know they want to leave, they know they will leave, but they keep putting off the job search. Meanwhile back at the desk, the job deteriorates until you reach the breaking point.

Now you need another job and you need it in a hurry. So you take the first decent position that comes along. It wasn't what you were looking for, but you were desperate. Result: Another couple of frustrating years until the cycle starts all over again.

Actually, we believe you should change horses *while* your current position is still fun. When you do it this way, you're making a move from strength and not from weakness. Some people, however, need to feel bad before they are motivated enough to move on. If you think you fit this description, there's a way to kick yourself out of the nest.

Ask yourself, "Am I going to be working for this company five years from now?" If your answer is "Definitely yes," then you have found your horse. You should ride that horse for all it's worth.

If your answer to the question is "Definitely no," then you shouldn't wait around and waste another five years. Start looking for a replacement horse right away.

Take your time. Don't rush things. Your current position is still fun, right? So you can afford the luxury of keeping your options open, not jumping at the first offer. Remember, however, you're not looking for a job; you're looking for a horse. There's a big difference.

A job is a position with duties, hours, salary, medical benefits, pensions, perks. A horse is an idea, a product, a person. When you fill a job, you are putting yourself on the line to perform specific services. When you ride a horse, you are casting your lot with someone or something outside of yourself. What you wind up doing might be totally different from what you first imagined. Who cares, as long as the horse ends up taking you on a terrific ride?

It's better to be a dishwasher for a winner than the captain of the Titanic.

Suppose your answer to the question "Am I going to be working for this company five years from now?" is "Maybe." (Don't worry. That's not an uncommon answer.) Then you should act as if you won't be working for your present company in five years. Keep your eyes open and look around.

If you study the careers of highly successful people, you'll find an enormous amount of mental flexibility. They are able not just to recognize a good opportunity, but to take decisive action to seize the opportunity before it blows away. Saddest of all are the people who seem to be frozen in time. Nothing good ever happens to them because they seem to be unwilling to change. Recently the director of alumni affairs at Harvard's prestigious John F. Kennedy School of Government left to become a manager of the pop group New Kids on the Block. This may not turn out to be a good move, but you know the person has the mental flexibility needed for a big winner. We don't recommend that you be a job-hopping butterfly, flitting from one firm to another, although it is true that many highly successful people started their careers with a rapid succession of jobs. What made them highly successful was the fact that they stuck around when they found the right job. It's not your first job that makes you a winner. It's your last one.

When you do leave, don't burn your bridges behind. You never know. Maybe the situation will change. New management could move in and want you back, at a big increase in salary and an interesting horse to ride.

How do you recognize the conditions that create opportunities for changing horses? Here are some guidelines.

When a new industry emerges

Back in 1983, when the personal computer industry was starting to boom, Jan Nygren sold her piano and bought a PC. She's now president of Computer Basics, Inc., one of Long Island's leading computer instruction firms.

Nygren was a school teacher in Glen Cove when she discovered the world of computers. Specifically, she explored the ways that computers could help children. Soon she turned her garage into a studio and began conducting her own workshops. Today computers have become a primary focus of her life (right after her family, she says). She attends seminars and conferences the world over.

Could you do the same thing today that Jan Nygren did in 1983? Sure, you could sell your piano and buy a computer, but you probably wouldn't be able to build a business with it. The personal computer window of opportunity is pretty much closed.

When a new industry emerges, most people shy away from it. They have no experience in the new industry. But don't forget: nobody else does either. Which is why a new industry represents such a golden opportunity.

Jim Manzi bounced around for a few years before he hit pay dirt. After graduating from Colgate University in 1973, he studied classics at Columbia. After 12 weeks of Plato and Aristotle, he joined *National Review* magazine to research a book on the United Nations for William Buckley, Jr. In 1974 he moved to the Port Chester (New York) *Daily Item,* where he won awards for his articles on a village clerk who fixed bids on contracts. Three years later, while studying at Tufts University, Manzi decided to become a businessman. Unsure of what industry to enter, he joined McKinsey & Co. as a consultant. In 1982 he was assigned to the team that was developing a business plan for Lotus Development Corp., the publisher of the 1-2-3 spreadsheet software.

In 1983 Manzi joined Lotus to head up marketing and sales. In 1984 he was named president. In 1986 chairman and CEO. In 1987 his salary and stock options earned him $26.3 million, making him one of America's best compensated chief executives.

Jim Manzi was then 35 years old. His success is all the more memorable for someone who had never programmed a computer and had no management experience when he joined Lotus. But then, no one else had very much either. The personal computer industry was just getting off the ground.

Harold Katz was 34 years old in 1971 when he founded Nutri/System. He never went to college and had no experience in the weight-loss business. (He had worked in his father's grocery store and had sold insurance.) What he did have was motivation. He had spent years watching his own mother struggle with her weight. He also had a gimmick: his company charged customers hefty upfront fees, depending on the amount of weight they wanted to lose. (Who could resist the temptation to name a big number?)

Ten years later, Katz took Nutri/System public. By 1983 the company had 680 centers in 50 states. Katz was rich. He owned 65 percent of the shares, giving him a net worth on paper of some $300 million. Then the bottom fell out. But that's another story we will tell in the next chapter.

When the competitive situation changes

In the early days of a new industry, there is a lot of shifting back and forth. Companies rise and fall until finally the industry shakes down into a pecking order that endures for an extended period of time.

The personal computer industry is no different. Soon after the MITS Altair appeared on the January 1975 cover of *Popular Electronics*, there were five machines on the market. In addition to the Altair, the competitive machines included the Apple II, Commodore Pet, IMSAI 8080, and Radio Shack TRS-80.

Apple has become a dominant force in the personal

computer field. Commodore and Radio Shack have become niche players. That leaves MITS Altair and the IMSAI 8080, which took an interesting turn.

IMSAI was a creation of Bill Millard, an ex-IBM salesman who had started a computer consulting group. At one point in time, IMSAI actually seized the sales lead from MITS but soon fell behind. Millard was not a computer expert; he was a salesman.

One day an outsider, John Martin, approached Millard with an idea. Why not set up an organization to franchise computer stores? Sell franchises to dealers for $10,000 to $15,000 apiece, sell them IMSAI computers, and then collect 5 percent of everything the dealers sell.

Millard bought the idea and ComputerLand was born. When IBM introduced the PC in August 1981, ComputerLand became the first retailer to sell it. Along the way, the IMSAI organization disappeared and ComputerLand took its place. Millard had effectively switched horses from computers to computer retailing.

Bill Millard threw in the towel in 1987 and moved to Saipan. Before leaving the country, he sold his 52 percent of ComputerLand for about $80 million. Not a bad take for ten years of work.

When the company situation changes

Nimbleness is an asset almost everywhere, but especially when you work for a big company. You can be shot out from under your horse almost anytime.

Donald Brennan, at the age of 39, was vice chairman and heir apparent to Edwin Gee at International

Paper. When the board passed him over in 1982 in favor of another man, Brennan promptly changed horses and took a job in Morgan Stanley's paper advisory group. He's done well. Today he heads the merchant banking business at Morgan Stanley. In 1989 he earned at least $7 million.

Most managers in Brennan's shoes would have waited it out at International Paper. Maybe the new president will fall on his face. "I'll just wait around and see if he stubs his toe" is the typical attitude. Not a good strategy. If you wait around after someone decides not to give you the job you wanted, you give them a second chance not to give you the job you wanted.

If at first you don't succeed, change horses. Don't give management a second chance to make a dumb promotion.

Alan Lesk had spent half his lifetime working for Maidenform Inc. At the age of 48, he was senior vice president of sales and merchandising for the $200 million company. He looked forward to the day when the company's 73-year-old chairman, Beatrice Coleman, would name her successor. ("I dreamed I was president of Maidenform bra.")

That dream came true on September 25, 1989 ... but not for Alan Lesk. The mantle fell on Robert Brawer, another vice president. Brawer also had the advantage of being Ms. Coleman's son-in-law. Three days later Lesk left for another job.

"Life is unfair," said John Fitzgerald Kennedy. Life in a big corporation is even more unfair. And life in a family corporation is almost impossible unless your family name is on the door.

When that once-in-a-lifetime opportunity strikes

In 1984 Robin De Graff was a 27-year-old secretary to the plant manager at Extol of Ohio, an insulation fabricating company in Sandusky. Today the manager works for her. She owns the plant.

When Extol's owners put the plant up for sale in 1984, De Graff persuaded corporate executives to allow her to make the first bid. They agreed, provided she could find the financing.

Five banks rejected her. But the sixth bank put up just under $100,000. Since De Graff took over, she has more than doubled sales, to $1.7 million a year. The company is also expanding, recently buying a facility in Houston.

When that once-in-a-lifetime opportunity comes along, take it. Don't sit back and say, "I'm only 27. Maybe I should get some more experience before I take on such a big responsibility."

Just do it. The next once-in-a-lifetime opportunity might not arrive until your next lifetime.

Tony Ryan had an unimpressive 16-year career as a middle manager for Aer Lingus. Then in 1975, when violence in Northern Ireland pummeled passenger traffic, the airline asked him to try to lease its idle planes. Business was so good that Ryan decided to launch his own venture, the GPA Group.

With $50,000 in capital and the contacts his Aer Lingus assignment had provided, Ryan went to work. Today the GPA Group has 213 planes and $1 billion in annual revenues. Recently he announced plans to buy 308 jets for $16.8 billion, the largest plane order ever.

Tony Ryan is now one of Ireland's richest citizens, with a net worth of about $200 million.

Lew Frankfort was commissioner of New York City's Agency for Child Development when he ran into the founder of Coach Leatherware. Frankfort had helped save the city's Head Start program during the fiscal crisis of the mid-seventies.

Frankfort joined Coach as vice president for special projects. In 1985 he became president. Since taking over at Coach, Frankfort has quintupled sales to $100 million.

When you have fallen into a rut

Herman Cain was a "computer jock" who worked his way up to vice president, corporate systems and services, Pillsbury Company. With a staff job and no operating experience, he was unlikely to go any higher.

So at the age of 36, Cain started work at Burger King, a Pillsbury subsidiary, as a broiler crew member. (Sometimes you have to take a step down in order to move up.) In two months he became a restaurant manager and in nine months a regional vice president.

Cain went on to become president of Godfather's Pizza, another Pillsbury subsidiary. In 1988 Cain teamed up with other senior executives to lead a leveraged buyout of Godfather's. Total elapsed time from flipping burgers to primary owner of a 500-unit pizza chain: six years. That's fast even for the fast-food business.

Paul Roman was in a rut. At 41 he was working in

public relations for General Electric. (At 41 Jack Welch was a GE sector executive one step from the top.) Roman's career definitely wasn't on the fast track.

Roman was also frustrated at home. He was trying to build some bookshelves but found his progress stymied by the lack of high-quality instructions. An idea popped into his head. He would start a quality woodworking magazine with his wife Jan.

Before Paul quit General Electric, the Romans plowed all of their savings ($12,800) into a test mailing of a magazine called *Fine Woodworking*. Bingo! A 15 percent response proved they had a winner.

Today their company, Taunton Press, publishes *Fine Woodworking* and four other magazines with a total circulation of almost 900,000, plus books and videotapes. Taunton, owned outright by the Romans, has 200 employees and $25 million in revenues. Profits before taxes are at least $3 million a year. (Welch earned only $2.6 million last year.)

One reason for the Romans' success was their willingness to gamble. When they took a flier on *Fine Woodworking*, they had five young children to support.

Fear of change

Probably the No. 1 reason that keeps people from changing horses is a fear of the unknown. People hang on to a faltering horse because they can't quite deal with all the uncertainty of a new endeavor. With that point of view, it's easy to rationalize hanging on and doing nothing. Then one day your horse dies underneath you, and you've got nothing else to ride. But fear not and read on. Now that you know what's holding you back, you've still got time to make that move. But first be aware of the different kinds of fear to watch out for if you're contemplating a change.

The primary fear is that your new horse won't carry you very far. (What if my new venture fails?) So what? You try again. History is loaded with examples of people who ran up a long list of failures before they found that hot horse. And besides, your present horse could also fail you. In this day and age of corporate takeovers, mergers, failures, you name it, there are no guaranteed rides.

Another insidious fear is one in which a potential career change could bring with it a perceived loss of social status. In other words, if I trade my corporate executive horse to run a local business horse, will I be asked to resign from the country club? What do I say at the cocktail party when someone asks, "What do you do?"

Well, first you have to recognize that happiness is a lot more satisfying than status. We know a corporate executive who traded in his pinstripes for a local discount muffler franchise. He couldn't be happier. Not only does he make a lot more money, but he has escaped all the corporate politics that had been eating his stomach. When asked what he does now, he has two answers, depending on his mood and the company. At a fancy affair he simply bills himself as an investor. (Recently, in a muffler franchise.) In a more down-to-earth setting, he's an entrepreneur. Today that's a very hot occupation.

People are prone to get into comfortable ruts.

Life is predictable. You tend to know what to expect. Your experience makes things easy and quick.

Change, on the other hand, means that you'll have to work harder, learn new tricks, cope with the unexpected. You get anxious just thinking about all that change. Suddenly you have a bad case of the "what ifs." You're paralyzed. You stay put.

We have a certain empathy for this type of fear. We suffered from exactly this fear for many years as we rode our advertising agency horse.

Yes, dear readers, we're not as smart as we make out. We learned our lessons the hard way by not having enough courage to overcome our fear of change. It took us years to change horses. Maybe a little history is in order.

In the late sixties we were a young advertising agency climbing the ladder to fame and glory. Then we had what we thought was a big idea: focus on "strategy" instead of the agency mainstay of "creativity." So we developed a body of thought to demonstrate our strategic ability. "Positioning" was born. It was *our* horse, but we didn't have the courage to get off our agency horse. We rode on in the advertising business.

As the years went by, "Positioning" became a buzzword. We added another body of thought called "Marketing Warfare." And still we clung to our agency, hoping against hope that all this would result in more and bigger advertising accounts.

It never happened. Our agency was going nowhere. But slowly we began to notice that more and more folks were calling us about strategy instead of advertising. Did we see the light and change horses? Nope, we lumbered on and added yet another strategic body of thought, "Bottom-Up Marketing."

Then one day after our latest body of thought was

published in book form, your two stalwart authors finally screwed up their courage. We decided that since our last effort hadn't improved our advertising business, we were going to change horses. This meant getting rid of our advertising accounts, our staff, our New York City office. In short, we had to overcome our fear of change.

We did it at long last. We climbed aboard our "Positioning" horse, moved to Greenwich, Connecticut, became marketing strategists, and lived happily ever after. (So far.)

We should have started to ride the marketing strategy horse 20 years ago. Maybe you can profit from our mistakes.

Changing horses is never easy. There is no guarantee that the grass will actually be greener on the other side of the paddock. But if you're in a rut, you have no choice. Look around you, pick the horse with the most potential, cross your fingers, and climb into the saddle.

It may just be the best ride of your life.

14

There are
no second acts

"There are no second acts in American lives," wrote
F. Scott Fitzgerald. Then he went to Hollywood and
proved it.

After building Nutri/System to a weight-loss powerhouse, Harold Katz went on to other things. He bought
an executive recruiting outfit, a cosmetics firm, and a
chain of figure salons. He also tried to launch a national
chain for cosmetic dentistry and for unisex hairstyling
(both unsuccessful). To top it off, he bought his hometown basketball team, the Philadelphia 76ers.

His office reflected Katz's new-found affluence. The
whole thing was done in mirrors and black marble. The
conference table was circled by high-backed chairs that
cost $1800 each. In the back was an apartment with a
Jacuzzi and a state-of-the-art stereo system.

It wasn't long before his cash cow, Nutri/System Inc.,
started to go dry. In one year, net income fell from a $13

million profit to a $17 million loss. The stock dropped from $48 a share to about $4. Katz sold out.

What happened to Harold Katz in Philadelphia is also happening to Donald Trump in New York. And for exactly the same reason. Success can turn a mind into mush.

The Trump trap

Successful people often fall into the Trump trap. They forget what made them successful in the first place.

They assume that 100 percent of their good fortune is due to their own efforts. They discount circumstances, luck, timing, other people.

The horse that took them to the top now disappears in a cloud of egocentricity. Instead of riding another horse, they start to ride themselves. They begin to think they can do no wrong. A raving egocentricity combined with nonstop diversification is a formula for disaster.

Owen Lipstein launched *American Health* magazine in 1982 at the age of 29. Believing that existing health magazines had little relevance for today's fitness freaks, he quickly built the magazine's circulation to a million. He also built a million-dollar reputation. "Mr. Lipstein," wrote *The New York Times*, "was one of the magazine industry's wonder kids of the eighties, a start-up artist who seemingly could do no wrong."

Three years after launching *American Health*, Lipstein bought *Mother Earth News*. In 1988 he bought controlling interest in *Psychology Today*. That same year, together with a partner, he launched *Smart* magazine.

A year later, Lipstein's publishing empire began to unravel. Money problems forced him to sell his crown jewel, *American Health,* to the Reader's Digest Association for more than $40 million. But before the sale could go through, the company was late publishing several issues of the magazine. The tarnished publication was finally sold to the Digest for $29.1 million, barely enough to cover his debts.

Meanwhile, *Psychology Today* suspended publication. *Mother Earth News* sustained a sharp drop in ad pages. And *Smart* was put on the auction block. "Near-death is character-improving," says Lipstein, who may have lost his money but not his sense of humor.

You can find candidates for the Trump trap by reading almost any daily newspaper. They're the ones who get the most publicity, usually highly favorable, as did Owen Lipstein and Harold Katz. They're the ones who do the radio talk shows and television interviews. Often described as "human perpetual-motion machines," they're into everything. If they don't fall into the Trump trap, they do fall into the cardiac trap.

Perception is not reality. Some of the biggest names are living on the edge of disaster, as was Donald Trump. Read between the lines. People who are really successful don't have to write books or go on television to tell you how successful they are. The art of the deal is keeping your mouth shut about what a good deal you made.

When you fall into the Trump trap, you start to believe in your ability to run anything. A hotel, a condominium, a shopping plaza, a gambling casino, a football team, an airline. You stop looking for horses to ride, because you've found the best possible horse of all: yourself.

It's tragic.

The second coming

For one reason or another, many successful entrepreneurs sell their first business and then, after several years of retirement, try to start a second one. It seldom works.

We call these organizations Act II companies. They frequently stay alive only with money transfusions from the founders. They almost never are as successful as the original. Frequently they are disasters.

Perot Systems Corp. is a typical Act II company. EDS (Electronic Data Systems) was Ross Perot's first company, which he founded in 1962 with $1000 in cash and sold to General Motors 22 years later for $2.5 billion.

What motivates a man who has accomplished as much as Ross Perot has to start a second company at the age of 58? Much of the press and many stock analysts chalk it up to "revenge, pure and simple," as one analyst put it. Perot, they say, is conducting a vendetta against General Motors. EDS has simply gotten in the way.

Some say jealousy. "For a great man to see something profit after he's thought it was totally dependent on him must be hard," says an EDS attorney. "It's a classic example of when a whole lot is not enough."

Some say greed. Perot himself predicts that Perot Systems will be a $1 billion company in 1998.

Some say it's his competitive spirit. When Perot's old company challenged him in court, he compared it to the sneak attack on Pearl Harbor and vowed to go after every contract EDS had. "It will be like turning a bunch of bulldogs loose on a bunch of poodles," he declared.

We say it's all foolishness. When Ross Perot started EDS, he filled a void. His was the first systems integration company. He virtually invented the industry. That was the Idea Horse he had chosen to ride.

Perot Systems Corp. has no unique idea, no unique service, no unique position. All that Perot Systems Corp. has is Ross Perot, but he left his horse back at EDS.

Herrell's Ice Cream is another Act II company. Steve Herrell also founded the much more successful and widely known company, Steve's Homemade Ice Cream. He sold Steve's in 1977 and took up piano tuning. Three years later, a month after his noncompete agreement with Steve's expired, he opened Herrell's.

After ten years, Herrell's is much smaller than Steve's and likely to remain so.

When Steve opened Steve's, he had a Product Horse to ride: the first homemade ice cream with "mix-ins," candy and nuts mixed in by hand. Herrell's has the original Steve, but unfortunately it also has a me-too reputation.

Another Steve created what's probably the most famous Act II company, NeXT Inc. Steve Jobs' first venture, of course, was Apple, the world's most successful personal computer company. When he left Apple, his stock was worth more than $100 million. The contrast between the two companies is striking.

Apple was started in a garage. NeXT was started in three white and sea-green buildings overlooking the San Francisco Bay.

Apple was started on a shoestring. NeXT was started with $10 million from Jobs, $10 million from IBM, $20 million from Ross Perot, and $100 million from Canon.

Apple was started in anonymity. NeXT was started in a blaze of publicity, the likes of which the computer world has never seen before and probably will never see again.

Apple was started with a Product Horse, the world's first "packaged" personal computer. NeXT is another workstation in a field pioneered by Sun, Apollo, and others.

An Act II company is an ego-driven encore performance designed to prove to the world that your Act I success was no fluke and that you are an exceptionally talented individual. Ironically, an Act II company tends to prove the opposite—that your Act I success was a lucky break.

Actually, an Act II company has a better chance for success if it comes off of a failure. Bill Millard's personal computer business was dying when he shifted his energies to his ComputerLand retail chain. Failure forces you to look outside of yourself. You don't want to repeat your mistakes, so you don't concentrate on yourself. You focus on the outside. With an element of luck, you can sometimes find a better horse to ride.

Success does just the opposite. It tends to internalize things. Think of Steve Jobs. With everyone patting him on the back, he couldn't help but believe that he was the crucial force in Apple's phenomenal track record. If he was the Entrepreneur of the Decade, why couldn't he repeat that success with NeXT?

The loss of his illusions may be even more painful than his monetary loss.

No matter how brilliant you may be, you can't make success happen. You have to find it. And the fact that you found it once doesn't necessarily mean you can find it again, especially if you stop looking outside of yourself.

When you attribute your success solely to your own efforts, as Jobs apparently did, then you approach Act II with a superabundance of self-confidence and no horse sense. The seeds of many Act II failures are sown in the successes of Act I. The only things that grow are the egos involved.

Yet it is possible to go from one success to another. Many people have done it. When you study their histories, you usually find they found another angle for their second victory. They didn't depend on the momentum of Act I.

Jeno Paulucci did it. He made his first fortune with a new food concept—packaged chow mein. That was Chun King, which he sold to R. J. Reynolds for $63 million. He made his second fortune with Jeno's pizza rolls, which he sold to Pillsbury for $150 million.

The success of Chun King didn't make Paulucci believe he was a Chinese food expert. "I can do anything Chinese and be successful," an egocentric person might have interpreted the Chun King episode. Rather, Paulucci looked for another horse to ride and found it in a new food concept called "pizza rolls."

Most Act II ventures are run by people who try to stick to what worked the first time around, only this time they try to do it bigger and better than ever. That's

what gets a person into trouble. There's no more horse
to ride.

Why it's usually harder the second
time around

It shouldn't be. You approach Act II with a lot more of
everything than you had when you started Act I. More
confidence, more experience, more contacts, and most
important of all, more money. All of these things
should make the job easier. But they don't.

You tend to get blindsided by an excess of self-
confidence. If you think you are a winner, you don't
have to look outside of yourself for ways to win. You
just throw more of yourself into the project.

The saddest tales of all involve those people who
walk out on Act I because they blithely assume they can
always move on to Act II. They don't do it for the
money. Quite often, Act I has made them all the money
they will ever need.

Either they do it for the ego. (They will prove to the
world that they were the key ingredient in the success
of Act I.) Or they do it, quite frankly, just to have something to do.

We have witnessed many entrepreneurs embarking
on an Act II career. Loaded with money and oozing
self-confidence, they were blindly unaware of the problems to come. You won't necessarily read about their
troubles. If you have enough money to start with, it's
easy to lose a few million and never make the papers.
Old entrepreneurs don't die; they just fade away.

Act I for Fred and Gale Hayman was an enormously
successful perfume (and retail store in Beverly Hills)

called Giorgio. Interestingly enough, the Haymans did not create the scent. It had already been rejected by Revlon, Helena Rubenstein, and Yves St. Laurent before it was offered to the Haymans. (The ability to recognize a good idea or product is more important to success than the ability to create one.)

Hayman's gimmick was to make everyone aware of the perfume with massive advertising and then let hardly anyone sell it, creating instant demand. Giorgio quickly became the top-selling perfume in America.

But the Haymans, who were separated when they launched the perfume, went through a divorce and subsequently a custody battle over their offspring, Giorgio. To settle the battle, they sold out to Avon in 1987 for $165 million.

But the battle of Beverly Hills wasn't over. Both Haymans launched Act II perfumes. Fred was creative and called his brand "273," the address of his Rodeo Drive store. Gale simply called her brand "Beverly Hills." Who will win the second battle of Beverly Hills and who will lose?

Avon will likely win because it owns the first horse. Both Haymans will likely lose.

It won't be from lack of effort, at least in Fred Hayman's case. He introduced 273 with a party in typical excessive Hollywood style. A marching band played outside in the parking lot. A 100-piece mariachi band played inside for the partygoers. Fifty pounds of caviar was served on silver trays, wiping out several generations of sturgeon. Marvin Hamlisch wrote a song for the event, and Marilyn McCoo was the emcee.

Why go back to the well again when you're not thirsty? "I never felt I'd made it," says Fred Hayman.

"Not even when I cashed out." (He was 62 when he sold Giorgio.)

Ego is the root of all Act II disasters. You may have to prove it to yourself, but not to your friends and associates who assume you can do it again. Doing a thing once is plenty of proof and a lot more elegant. One spectacular success like Giorgio should have provided enough ego and monetary satisfaction to last a lifetime. You don't have to prove you can do it again.

If you find yourself in Fred or Gale's shoes, consider a compromise that will satisfy both parties. Like war itself, when disagreements escalate into open warfare, both sides invariably lose.

What the Haymans did for perfume, Mitch Kapor did for computer software with Lotus 1-2-3. As a young computer programmer, he went to work for the company that developed VisiCalc, the epoch-making spreadsheet program for the Apple computer. Kapor had an idea for an integrated software program that combined a spreadsheet with a word processing and a data base function.

VisiCorp, the makers of VisiCalc, rejected Kapor's idea for 1-2-3 because the program would clash with its existing product, repeating the same pattern taken by earlier manufacturers when they were offered what became the Giorgio scent. (It bears repeating that recognizing a good idea, not dreaming one up, is the essence of success in life.)

So Kapor started Lotus Development Corp. and the rest is history—including 1-2-3, which became the world's best-selling software program. In a bit of irony, 1-2-3 took off, not because it was integrated, but because it was the first spreadsheet program for the IBM PC.

In all probability, Kapor's conflict with Jim Manzi could have been resolved with a shuffling of responsibilities. In any event, he left Lotus to regain a sense of balance in his life. "A commitment to innovation," said Kapor, "kind of gets ground into hamburger in the gigantic meat grinder of corporate life."

After a year off to recharge his batteries, Kapor set up ON Technology, a new software company. It took almost three years and $9 million for ON's first product to get out the door. Called On Location, the new software product helps Macintosh users find files faster. Not exactly a blockbuster software product.

When you find a superior horse, it pays to figure out ways to stay on board. Starting over again is exceedingly difficult.

Paul Allen, cofounder of Microsoft with Bill Gates, left the company in 1983 to fight Hodgkin's disease. Two years later, after conquering his problem, he started a software company called Asymetrix Corp. Chances are, Asymetrix won't make many waves.

Mike Markkula, the invisible third partner of Steve Jobs and Steve Wozniak at Apple Computer, founded Echelon Corp. in 1988 with $30 million in venture capital. The company has come up with computer chip designs to make smart homes, smart factories, and smart cars possible at an affordable price. Chairman of the new company is Kenneth Oshman, who cofounded Rolm Corp. So Echelon really represents two Act II ventures, not a good sign.

Wozniak, who left Apple with a net worth of $45 million, recently shut down CL-9 Inc., a company he started in 1985 to make wireless remote control devices. Presumably, he still has most of his $45 million left.

Nolan Bushnell founded Atari and launched a whole new industry. Since he sold the video game giant in 1976, he's had more than his share of failures including Chuck E. Cheese Pizza Time Theater, which went belly up and lost nearly $100 million. "I'm not half back to where I was," says Bushnell today.

When Peter Goldmark, inventor of the long-playing record, turned to television, it was a different story. His CBS color television system, which was not compatible with black and white, lost out to the RCA development, which was.

When Edwin Land, inventor of the instant camera, turned to motion pictures, his Polavision system was a $100 million dud.

A failure is a success without the timing

One reason Act II efforts usually turn out poorly is their timing. A person will embark on Act II using exactly the same strategies that worked for Act I, only bigger and better. (Fred Hayman is a typical example.) The only difference is the timing.

Timing makes all the difference in the world. You cannot turn the clock back. John Young Brown, Jr., tried to repeat his Kentucky Fried Chicken success with H. Salt's English Fish and Chips. (He paid Haddon Salt $12 million for his company.)

"John was trying to clone Kentucky Fried," said one of his executives. "He had done so well with chicken, he thought he could use the same techniques, the same procedures, and duplicate the experience with roast beef or fish or whatever. The trouble was that he didn't have a Colonel for fish or roast beef. And he wasn't the first in the field."

Walter Mack, the legendary genius who built Pepsi-Cola into a major contender in the field in the thirties and forties, launched King Cola in 1978. In spite of the fact that Mack was 83 years old at the time, the press gave King Cola a reasonable chance for success. Three years later the company was bankrupt.

Kemmons Wilson, the founder of Holiday Inns, recently introduced two new lodging chains: Wilson World hotels and Wilson Inns. Prognosis: Not good. Holiday Inn was the first modern "hotel" alternative to the "Cozy Cabins" that used to line the roadsides of America. Neither Wilson World hotels nor Wilson Inns are a "first."

Norman Lear, who revolutionized television with the hit series *All in the Family*, has just launched a media and entertainment empire called Act III Communications Inc. He has borrowed heavily to buy three theater chains, eight television stations, and 12 trade magazines. Act III, a name presumably chosen to celebrate Lear's movement from writer to producer to mogul, is off to a rocky start. At the age of 67, Lear has even bigger plans in mind. "This is a Shakespearean play," he quips. "Those have five acts." We wonder.

W. Michael Blumenthal had a spectacular career at Bendix capped by a term as U.S. Treasury secretary under President Jimmy Carter. After being named chief executive of Bendix at age 46, he turned the conglomerate around, becoming one of the country's best-known and best-respected executives in the process. Act II has not been so kind to Mr. Blumenthal. First he took a job with Burroughs Corporation. Then he engineered the 1986 merger between Burroughs and Sperry, which became the Unisys Corporation. After saying repeatedly he would not retire until Unisys was a big success, he announced his retirement in January 1990 on a day when Unisys reported an 84 percent drop in fourth-quarter net income and a $639 million loss for the year.

Harry Gray, retired chairman of United Technologies Corporation, just took over as chief executive of American Medical International. At the age of 70, Mr. Gray has his hands full with a sick $3 billion company. Revenues are declining and the company is losing money.

Repeating Act I

While there are few examples of successful Act IIs, there are many people who have come back to successfully repeat Act I. In 1985 Sandra Kurtzig quit the software company she had started at her kitchen table 13 years earlier and set off on personal pursuits: building a house in Hawaii, writing an autobiography, and spending more time with her two sons. In 1989, with earnings slipping, she returned.

Kurtzig's company is no small potatoes. Her $200 million-a-year ASK Computer Systems has 55 offices worldwide and nearly 1000 employees. We expect it to resume its rapid growth. "Founders are the best flag carriers," said a venture capitalist about Ms. Kurtzig's return.

A. W. Clausen, chief executive of BankAmerica, left in 1981 to head up the World Bank. In a few years, massive loan losses and ballooning expenses caused BankAmerica to come close to collapse. Mr. Clausen returned in 1986 and turned the bank around. Today profits are soaring.

In 1983 Phil Knight left Nike, the running shoe company he cofounded. The next year profits promptly fell 29 percent, the first drop in ten years. Mr. Knight returned. Today Nike is the best-selling athletic footwear brand in the world. Founders are the best flag carriers.

In 1979 John Koss hired a professional manager to run his family business. (Koss is the pioneer who developed the first audio headsets for the home market.) He sat back and gave the manager carte blanche to expand the business. The result was line extension and diversification that ultimately put Koss Corp. into Chapter 11.

In 1984 Koss took over again. "I should have trusted my instincts," said John Koss, "but I figured I didn't have a college degree so who was I to question MBAs?" Today Koss Corp. is once again a successful family business run by a father with help from two sons and two sons-in-law. It no longer employs a professional manager.

15

Excuses, excuses

Many people are better at finding excuses than at finding a horse to ride. When opportunity knocks, and it always does, you have to be ready to ride. You have only yourself to blame if you hide behind one of these excuses.

"I'm too old."
"I'm too young."
"I'm too shy."
"I'm not smart enough."
"I'm too lazy."
"I'm too poor."
"I'm too late."

The truth of the matter is that it is a big world out there and, in terms of opportunity, it's getting bigger all the time. Beneath the relatively few names that you read about in the newspapers or see on television, there are armies of very successful people riding all kinds of horses in all walks of life.

If you have any doubts, just stroll around some of the marinas that can be found in liberal supply around the world. The number of big boats that populate these floating cities never ceases to amaze us. You have to say that just in terms of big boats, there are many more successful people than the few you read about.

If you can't find a marina, just drive through some of the high-rent districts in America. Take a look at the big homes you find there.

While you're driving around the high-rent districts, count the Mercedes, BMWs, and Jaguars you see. Last year alone, Americans bought 159,562 of these luxury cars.

But what's even more illuminating is to ask a few questions about the owners of these boats and cars and homes. What you get back isn't the fact that the owner is the CEO of some *Fortune* 500 corporation. Nine times out of ten you'll hear that the owner did something like invent a medical testing device or a coin changer. Or distributes something exciting like plumbing supplies.

Some of the success stories will amaze you. In Colorado you'll find a ranch that isn't raising cattle. It's raising elk. The reason: they're a lot more profitable. A breeding female elk, for example, goes for $7000. (Here's a case where someone found an elk to ride.)

America is a land of opportunity because we're a society with an enormous infrastructure comprised of thousands of very successful ideas, services, and products being sold or invented by people you've never heard of. Nor ever will.

Horses abound. Furthermore, there's a shortage of horse sense. You just have to get out of yourself and look around. That said, here are some guidelines to keep in mind as you search for that mount.

1. Personality is more important than intelligence

When you live in a world that has 5 billion people, it's pretty apparent that you have to learn to get along with folks if you want to get ahead. And with those kinds of numbers, the law of averages is against you when it comes to being smarter than the rest.

It's better to be a charmer than a smart-ass.

Personality is an enormous asset in the success game. Not just because people think you're funny or charming or gracious. It's because people with personality are by nature focused outside of themselves. Their energies are directed toward others and the way things are.

Intelligence, on the other hand, tends to focus people on themselves and their view of the world, which is often based on the way they wish things to be. Highly intelligent people tend not to have a realistic view of the world. Everything gets screened through their egos. That often leads to their misjudging opportunities. Since revolutionary ideas often seem foolish at first, intelligent people miss a lot of them.

If you have any doubt about the power of charm, just read *The Wall Street Journal*. At least once a month you'll read about some con man who charmed millions of dollars out of some greedy but unsuspecting investors.

2. In the purest democracy, there will never be equality of opportunity

Some people are born with the right parents. Others are born in the right decade. Still others are born in the right location.

If you were blessed with none of these natural advantages, then you must create your own edge by finding a horse to ride. If you try to win the race for success all by yourself, you start with a serious handicap. The mere fact that you decide to find a horse instead of staking everything on yourself gives you an enormous advantage. Most people don't.

Envy can be a big roadblock to those who want to use the "lack of opportunity" excuse.

This type of person tends to focus on other people's horses and how successfully they are riding them. Envious people like this go through life talking about how well Mr. X is doing or how lucky Ms. Y has become and how unlucky they are for a variety of reasons. As a result, they don't spend enough time focusing on something for themselves to ride.

3. Let go of your dreams—seize the opportunity when it appears

There are literally thousands of actors and actresses in Hollywood who dream of being a big star. Very, very few ever make it. Most people live the life of the big dream. It nurtures them, sustains them, and ultimately fails them. To be a big success, you have to find the dream outside of yourself. There are literally thousands of Success Horses to ride. Let go of your dream and open your eyes.

The trouble with dreams is that they tend not to be real. They are figments of your imagination. Horses run in the real world.

Anything that becomes a big deal starts out as a small deal. Dreams always start as a big deal. As a result, the dreamer loses touch with the reality of what it takes to ride and nurture a horse along the slow but steady path to success. And "slow" is the word.

Things that become successful too quickly often turn into a fad. What goes up like a rocket comes down like a rocket. People involved with a fad start to live and believe in the dream, and once again they lose touch with the real world.

The sad saga of Donald Trump is a case in point. He had a family to ride, which he did with great success. But he also had a dream of wealth and power. Soon the dream took over and he began to believe all his press clips. His ego took charge. He lost touch with the real world. He lost a lot of money en route. His dream was shattered on the rocks of reality.

4. Career planning is an exercise in delusion

One of the great myths in Corporate America is career planning. Young people envision a land of human resources managers carefully guiding their steps up the corporate ladder. As they go up the ladder of success, they are nurtured, trained, loved, and promoted.

Forget it.

No one knows the future. All we know is the past. Predicting the future is an exercise in delusion. It's like riding a race horse backwards.

Career planning at General Foods became a little tricky when the company was bought by Philip Morris.

Career planning at Wang became a problem when the personal computer overtook the word processor and put the company right at the edge of disaster.

And speaking of computers, career planning at IBM is no longer easy when the company is trying to reduce its work force by 10,000 people.

Your best bet in an ever-changing world is to cling to that horse for all you're worth. Riding is better than planning.

5. It's never too early— it's never too late

Bill Gates was a teenager at Harvard when he found the Software Horse to ride. So he quit school to build the company that became Microsoft.

Ray Kroc was 51 years old before he saw his first McDonald's restaurant. Harvey Mackay was 54 before he wrote his first book. Harlan Sanders was 65 before he sold his first Kentucky Fried Chicken franchise.

Success knows no age.

Obviously, it's a little better to find your horse at an early age since you'll be able to have a longer ride. But sometimes it takes a while before you find an opportunity to jump aboard.

A youthful mind is also an advantage because it tends to be more open to new ideas and trends. Youth is quite willing to challenge conventional wisdom and go against the grain. This kind of thinking is very useful in finding a horse.

The older mind tends to be less flexible and loaded down with conventional wisdom. That's why it's important for this type of mind to work at staying open. If you're a little older, make sure you spend some time with the younger generation. Keep up with the trends.

But more than anything else, an older person has to

be willing to drop everything when that horse appears. (Obviously, this is not a problem for a younger person who has little to drop.) Ray Kroc left his job of selling restaurant equipment to found McDonald's. Herb Kelleher dropped his legal profession to found Southwest Airlines.

When it's time to climb aboard, you can't take along a lot of life's accumulated baggage.

6. A closed mouth gathers no foot

Most people can't wait to express their opinions in order to impress their friends and associates. Hold your thoughts. Wait until others express their ideas first. It's a lot easier to find a horse to ride with an open mind and a closed mouth than it is with a closed mind and a motor mouth.

If you want to be considered a genius among friends and acquaintances, practice saying "That's interesting" with emotion and feeling.

This idea reinforces the earlier principle about the importance of personality over intelligence.

When people are comfortable with you, they tend to open up and tell you more. And since you're not talking, you get a chance to listen. And listening is critical when you're trying to find that horse to ride.

We'll let you in on a little trade secret of ours. When we're doing marketing consulting with big companies on what idea or horse that company should ride, the answer usually comes out of the mouths of the people who hired us to find the solution. The answer or horse is there. It's just that it's too obvious. No one can see it. They're all too busy going to meetings and talking.

So it is in life. If you listen and watch, you're in a better position to see the obvious. If you're busy pontificating, your chances of seeing things clearly are diminished. It's hard to observe and talk at the same time.

7. Look for your horse on the frontier

Why do we have a lot of computer examples in this book? Because computers and computer software are the new frontier. Opportunities are almost always on the new frontier. It's the frontier that creates the opportunities, not you. However, for you, computers might not be the new frontier, because they are yesterday's frontier. For you the question is, What's the frontier of the future?

That's the first thing you have to ask yourself. Not what do I want to do? What am I like? Who am I? What am I?

Forget yourself. What is the frontier of the future? That's the question to ask. While no one knows the future, you can put yourself in the path of new ideas and new concepts as they develop. You always want to be where the action is taking place. You always want to be looking for a horse to ride.

So there you are. Stop making excuses. Get out there and find a horse. Hopefully, we have given you a better sense of how to find one.